Statistical Analysis Of American Divorce

STUDIES IN HISTORY, ECONOMICS AND
PUBLIC LAW

Edited by the

FACULTY OF POLITICAL SCIENCE
OF COLUMBIA UNIVERSITY

NUMBER 360

STATISTICAL ANALYSIS OF
AMERICAN DIVORCE

BY
ALFRED CAHEN

NEW YORK
COLUMBIA UNIVERSITY PRESS
LONDON: P. S. KING & SON, LTD.
1932

COPYRIGHT, 1932

BY

COLUMBIA UNIVERSITY PRESS

PRINTED IN THE UNITED STATES OF AMERICA

Dedicated

TO THE

MEMORY OF

MY FATHER

CONTENTS

PAGE

CHAPTER I

American Family Breakdown 15

CHAPTER II

Probability of Divorce. 21

CHAPTER III

Grounds for Divorce 32

CHAPTER IV

Underlying Conditions 45

CHAPTER V

Migratory Divorce 63

CHAPTER VI

Laws and the Home 79

CHAPTER VII

Remarriage. 98

CHAPTER VIII

Trends of the Vanishing Family. 110

CHAPTER IX

Persistent Causes 126

CHAPTER X

Dynamic Society and Divorce Velocity 138

BIBLIOGRAPHY 143

INDEX 147

LIST OF TABLES

			PAGE
TABLE	1.	States with Decreasing Divorce Rates.	25
TABLE	2.	Decennial Estimates of Divorce Frequency.	29
TABLE	3.	Percentage Distribution of Grounds of Divorce, 1867.	35
TABLE	4.	Percentage Distribution of Grounds of Divorce for Husband and Wife, 1928.	37
TABLE	5.	Refined Classification of Grounds of Divorce on Percentage Basis, 1928	41
TABLE	6.	Average Percentages Divorced of the Urban and Rural Racial Populations of the Five Selected States, 1920.	58
TABLE	7.	Percentage Distribution of Divorces According to Size of Family, 1928.	112
TABLE	8.	Divorce and Homeless Children in Portland, Oregon, 1921	115
TABLE	9.	Divorce in Relation to Duration of Marriage, 1928	120
TABLE	10.	Trends of Divorce and Four Related Economic and Social Factors.	130
TABLE	11.	Years of Declining Divorce Rates	135

LIST OF CHARTS

			PAGE
CHART	1.	Divorce Rates by States, 1870	22
CHART	2.	Divorce Rates by States, 1900	24
CHART	3.	Divorce Rates by States, 1929	26
CHART	4.	Map of States with Decreasing Divorce Rates Shown in White, 1929	28
CHART	5.	Century Race Between Death and Divorce. . . .	31
CHART	6.	Map Showing Prevalence of Divorce in Nine Geographical Sections of the Country, 1929	33
CHART	7.	Comparative Divorce Rates for the Nine Census Divisions of the Nation, 1929	34
CHART	8.	Distribution of Grounds for Divorce, 1867	36
CHART	9.	Distribution of Grounds for Divorce, 1928	38
CHART	10.	Standard Area Divorce Map 'of Thirty-nine States, 1929	52
CHART	11.	Per cent of Divorces Involving Children, 1928. . . .	111
CHART	12.	Probabilities of Divorce According to Presence or Absence of Children, 1928.	114
CHART	13.	Percentage Distribution of Divorces Granted in 1928 for First Thirty Years of Marriage.	117
CHART	14.	Relative Probabilities of Divorce and Death for First Thirty Years of Marriage, 1928	119
CHART	15.	Corrected Distribution Showing Probabilities of Divorce for First Thirty Years of Marriage, 1928.	122
CHART	16.	Length of Married Life till Death or Divorce, 1928. .	124
CHART	17.	Annual Fluctuations in Rates of Divorce and Economic Production on Ratio Scale	131
CHART	18.	Growth of Divorce and Four Related Factors on Ratio Scale	134

CHAPTER I

AMERICAN FAMILY BREAKDOWN

DURING the year 1929, 201,468 divorces were granted in the United States, or about one every two minutes. By calculations to be examined in a later chapter, it is evident that about 18 per cent of all American marriages, or more than one in every six, definitely ends in divorce. Over half a million men, women and children are directly affected every year by the grist of the divorce mill.

Divorce is legally defined in the United States as "the dissolution or suspension by law of marital relations." [1] The derivation of the word divorce comes from the Latin *diversae mentes,* or different minds. Both permanent divorces and also legal separations known as *divortium a mensa et thoro* or divorce from board and bed are included in the legal definition. The latter, however, are supposed to constitute a very small percentage of the total family disruptions, and in many states they automatically lapse into absolute divorces after a period of years.

Herbert Hoover, during his final presidential campaign speech in 1928, lauded the American home in the following tribute:

The unit of American life is the family. It is the economic unit as well as the moral and spiritual unit. But it is more than this. It is the beginning of self-government. It is the throne of our highest ideals. It is the source of the spiritual energy of our people. For the perfecting of this unit we must lend every energy of the government.

Two hundred thousand divorces do not measure the total

---

[1] *Corpus Juris* (New York, 1920), vol. xix, p. 16

16 STATISTICAL ANALYSIS OF AMERICAN DIVORCE

amount of American family breakdown. Studies in Philadelphia[2] and Chicago[3] showed that desertion, popularly known as the poor man's divorce, was prevalent among the foreign population and in slum districts. Desertion rivaled divorce in frequency of occurrence, and the inquiries further indicated that these two phases of marital disruption somewhat overlapped.

The most complete investigation of desertion was by Joanna C. Colcord for the Russell Sage Foundation[4] The facts evidenced that desertion is not the poor man's divorce since the deserter does not as a rule consider his absence from home as anything so final and definite as a divorce. The Philadelphia Society for Organizing Charity discovered that seven-eighths of deserting men had left their families more than once. The consensus of opinion of social workers seemed to be that desertion was merely the poor man's vacation.

There are accurate divorce statistics annually from the United States Bureau of the Census, but virtually no records exist concerning this troublesome problem of family desertion. In 1928 the National Desertion Bureau sent questionnaires to urban community organizations for Family Welfare, Child Care, Probation and Legal Aid.[5] To the question, " Is family desertion a vexing problem in your community? " 134 answers out of 145 replied affirmatively. Among 93 cities, desertion rates varied from 28 to 203 per 100,000 population. The report declares that the smaller cities present the larger desertion rates " probably due to the fact that

[2] Patterson, ' Family Desertion and Non-Support," *The Journal of Delinquency,* September, 1922, pp 262-264

[3] Mowrer, *Family Disorganization* (Chicago, 1927), pp 118-119

[4] Colcord, *Broken Homes* (Philadelphia, 1919), pp. 7-8.

[5] *Report of the Desertion Committee Compiled from the Questionnaires* (New York, 1928), mimeographed material.

AMERICAN FAMILY BREAKDOWN

only a part of the problem is encountered by those organizations recording from larger places. Probably the ratio for
the smaller cities more nearly represents the true ratio for all
places."

The report continues: "The urban population of the
United States in 1920 amounted to over 50,000,000 people.
With a probable 100 desertions per 100,000 population, the
total desertions in urban United States may be in excess of
50,000 annually"

This is simply an approximation of the numerical extent
of desertion. For 1929 there were actually 201,000 divorces
and over 4,000 annulments of marriage.[6] Fifty thousand
desertions cannot rightly be added to this total of family
wreckage, because as previously stated, many social workers
believe desertions are just temporary gaps in family relationships. Furthermore, some desertions of the permanent
type eventually are included among the divorces granted on
the legal ground of desertion. However, since 18 per cent
of American marriages are broken by divorce alone, President Hoover's idealistic picture of American family life deserves careful examination. The plain facts show that a
considerable proportion of American families is today
floundering between the rocks of divorce and desertion.

Divorce data are collected annually from the records of
county clerks, and the total number of divorces reported for
the country is substantially accurate. Unfortunately, the
records do not provide a very deep insight into the underlying causes of divorce. Questions on the census schedule
are brief and simple, merely giving the information:[7]

[6] Neither annulment nor desertion is an integral part of this study on
divorce. Annulment differs from divorce since the former purports
"fraud of some kind manifest in concealment by one or the other party
of a condition, which would have barred the marriage." *World Almanac*,
1928, p. 215.

[7] This and many of the later citations of facts and figures are from the
U. S. Marriage and Divorce Report, 1928, and previous annual issues.

18 STATISTICAL ANALYSIS OF AMERICAN DIVORCE

1. Legal ground upon which divorce was granted.
2. Was husband or wife the plaintiff?
3. Was the case contested?
4. The duration in years of the marriage.
5. The number of children.

These are the crude facts upon which a deeper analysis must be founded.

An inductive approach to this problem is aided by an historical background of American divorce statistics for several decades. Due primarily to the agitation of the National Divorce Reform League, which was organized under the leadership of President Woolsey of Yale University, as chairman, and the Reverend Dr. Samuel W. Dike as executive secretary, a marriage and divorce survey was strongly urged. Congress passed such a law, and in 1889 Dr. Carroll D. Wright, United States Commissioner of Labor, presented a monumental statistical document, *U. S. Marriage and Divorce Report*, 1867-1886. Through the influence of President Roosevelt the marriage and divorce records were later continued for the years 1887-1906 inclusive. Annual government reports were published for the year 1916 and for every individual year from 1922 to the last available figures of 1929. For the years between 1906 and 1922 the Census Bureau estimated the number of divorces from scattering reports of sixteen states. Thus there is virtually a continuous record of the progress of American divorce from the Civil War to the present time. The earlier years under-estimated the number of divorces perhaps 2 per cent,[8] while the present total of divorce is virtually complete, so the entire federal divorce reports present unusually high accuracy.

The statistical unit to be employed is divorce rate per

[8] Willcox, *The Divorce Problem, a Study in Statistics* (New York, 1891), p. 14.

AMERICAN FAMILY BREAKDOWN 19

thousand married population. For the year 1929 this rate was 4.05 divorces per thousand married people in the United States. Popular magazine writers often compare the number of divorces every year with the number of marriages. This is decidedly erroneous since there is no logical relationship between them, as extremely few marriages end in divorce the same year. The majority of writers on divorce accept the statistical unit, divorces per thousand of the total population. This is likewise fundamentally wrong for comparative purposes since only the married population accounts for divorces. A divorce rate based on a total population neglects entirely the changes from year to year in the number of marriages or in the age composition of the population. In comparison of divorce rates among the states, it also neglects the fact that some western states have a much lower percentage of the total population in the marital condition because of the disproportionate number of males living there. The only fair method for comparing divorce rates either by states or by years, therefore, seems to be the statistical unit, divorces per thousand married population. In order to evaluate the difference between a divorce rate based on the married population, and one based, according to common practice, on the total population, the usual statistical test for the significance of a difference was applied.[9] The result showed a fundamental divergence between the two groups, as is logically correct, since the standard unit, divorce rate based on the married population, alone takes into account major fluctuations of the marriage rate.

The same procedure is followed in the treatment of all topics. First, the opinions of authorities on the divorce

[9] The test for the standard error of the difference in the nine census divisions of the country showed the difference of the means to be 2.36 or more than three times the standard deviation, which is .76. See Chaddock, *Principles and Methods of Statistics* (Cambridge, Mass., 1925), pp. 239-240.

20 STATISTICAL ANALYSIS OF AMERICAN DIVORCE

problem are stated. Second the application of statistical methods to the numerical evidence on divorce and related economic and social data is explored. The final step is to test the hypotheses of experts and also those of a priori reasoning in order to derive conclusions on causes of increasing divorce.

The following three chapters describe the frequency of divorce in the United States with a detailed survey of its occurrence in various sections of the country. Chapters five, six and seven deal separately with some prominent aspects of the divorce situation to ascertain whether they effect rising divorce. The final three chapters analyze numerical data on associated economic and social factors in order to discover environmental forces in American life influencing the persistent advance of the divorce rate. The growing prevalence of family breakdown requires the careful application of statistical methods to this problem in social causation. The keen, clear penetration of quantitative analysis may help perhaps to explain some causes of increasing divorce.

CHAPTER II

Probability of Divorce

The number of divorces has increased from about 10,000 a year in 1867 to more than 200,000 in 1929. Population increased during that period about 300 per cent, marriages almost 400 per cent and divorces about 2,000 per cent. Thus the rate of divorce increase advanced about five times as rapidly as the proportion of married population in the United States over a period of 63 years.

It is remarkable that the actual divorce rate itself, based on the yearly ratio between divorces and the married population, has increased very uniformly every decade from the Civil War to the present time. A modified exponential curve fits the trend of the divorce rate excellently. In other words, the divorce rate has compounded annually at about a 3 per cent rate of increment since the years following the Civil War.

Despite the uniformity of its advance, the annual fluctuations have been most irregular. Even for such a comparatively stable period in American development as 1922 to 1928, the fluctuations of annual divorce rates indicate great instability.[1] This may point to a diversity of causes in the increase of American divorce. The uniformity of the increase by decades despite the irregularities in yearly oscillations of the divorce rate perhaps results from a fusion of compensating factors.

[1] A coefficient of disturbancy was calculated for divorce rates in those years compared to the ratio of the married population, showing $P = 8.57$, demonstrating a supernormal dispersion. See Rietz, *Handbook of Mathematical Statistics* (Cambridge, Mass., 1924), pp. 88-90.

STATISTICAL ANALYSIS OF AMERICAN DIVORCE

CHART 1

Divorce Rates by States, 1870

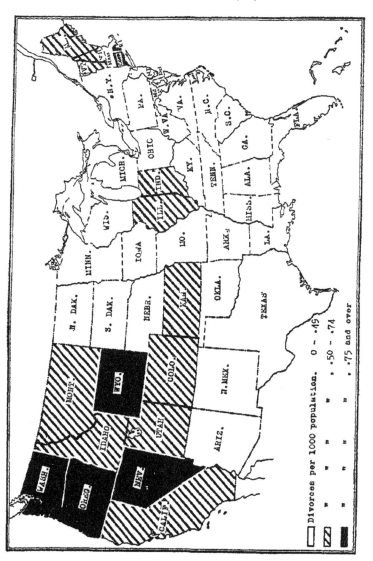

PROBABILITY OF DIVORCE

The same states and sections of the country have not produced uniform increases in divorce, resulting in the fivefold advancement of the national divorce rate for this entire period. Charts 1, 2 and 3 depict the rise of divorce for all the states in the years 1870, 1900 and 1929; the maps portray a mounting tide of divorce, but with western states usually predominating.[2] However, the same states have been far from uniform in their rates of increase for divorces. A coefficient of rank correlation was computed, comparing divorce rates by states for 1870 and 1929. The value of the coefficient, +.50, indicates that only about one-fourth of the leading divorce states of 1867 are still among the leaders in 1929.[3] The three maps do show that divorce rates have increased in virtually every state and section in the country. They represent divorce as a dark cloud of increasing density from East to West gradually gathering over the whole country from 1870 to 1929.

Almost twenty years ago Professor Edward A. Ross of Wisconsin University, and other sociologists, considered that this country was in a transitional period, so that the divorce rate would gradually reach a saturation point.[4] Nevertheless, the percentage of divorces has kept advancing at a rate 30 per cent a decade based on the married population. Professor William F. Ogburn of the University of Chicago believes that the factors which are causing a decline in the functions of the home, and therefore an increase in divorce,

---

[2] Divorce rates based on the total population were the only ones available for this special series.

[3] Since a coefficient of correlation varies between +1 and —1, a value of +.5 is not particularly high when based on a number so small as that of forty-eight states. The coefficient is squared to indicate proportionate relationship between two variables. See Ezekiel, *Methods of Correlation Analysis* (New York, 1930), p. 120.

[4] Ross, *Changing America* (New York, 1912), ch. iv.

24 STATISTICAL ANALYSIS OF AMERICAN DIVORCE

CHART 2

Divorce Rates by States, 1900

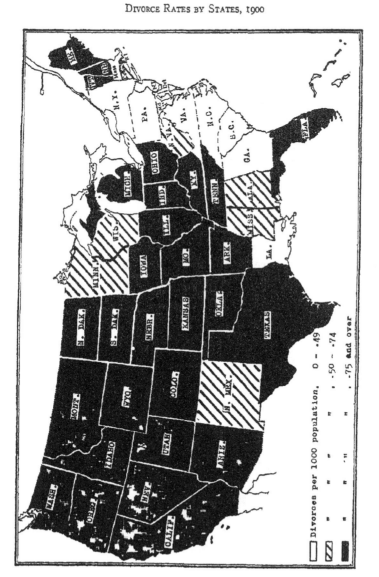

PROBABILITY OF DIVORCE

are still operating, and will continue to operate, with a consequent increase of divorce.   He writes:

Indeed there seems to be no sign of a slackening of the increase of divorce in the United States.   One wonders whether there is a natural limit.   Any natural or mathematical limit to the divorce rate seems far removed and it is quite conceivable that the increase may continue for some time.[5]

In order to discover whether there is any saturation point in the divorce rate of the United States which at present produces a marital fatality of 18 per cent, perhaps one should best examine the individual trends of the forty-eight divorce jurisdictions.   Only ten states had higher divorce rates some specific year before 1925 than they achieved during the five years since that date.   The map, Chart 4, shows in white the ten states in which the divorce rate has declined.   All other states have shown percentage increases in divorce. The following table gives the states with decreasing divorce, the year in which their highest divorce rate was achieved, and the percentage decline of the 1929 divorce rate from the year of greatest divorce frequency.

TABLE I.   STATES WITH DECREASING DIVORCE RATES

	Year of Highest Rate	Percentage Decline from given Year to 1929
New Hampshire	1923	11
Massachusetts	1924	9
Rhode Island	1924	19
Pennsylvania	1924	8
Delaware	1922	26
District of Columbia	1899	75
North Dakota	1900	6
Nebraska	1922	27
Louisiana	1922	9
Montana	1916	9

[5] Groves and Ogburn, *American Marriage and Family Relationships* (New York, 1928), p. 129.

CHART 3

Divorce Rates by States, 1929

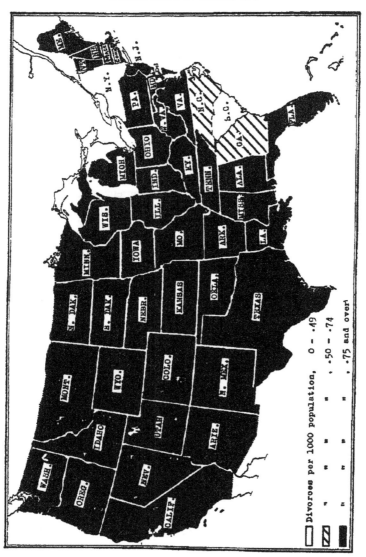

PROBABILITY OF DIVORCE

The areas of declining divorce are rather few and the decreases recorded comparatively small, with the exception of the District of Columbia. There the large reduction of the divorce rate occurred after a lobby had influenced Congress to reform the divorce law. Of the states showing decreases in divorce only two, Nebraska and Montana, were ever among the high divorce-producing states. Evidence from the remaining thirty-eight states thus seems to indicate that the American divorce rate still continues to maintain an upward secular trend. Great fear has often been expressed that the high divorce rate will eventually cause complete family breakdown and a national disaster.

There is nothing new about such alarming prophecies. Just a few years after the commencement of the American republic, the Reverend Benjamin Trumbull, President of Yale University, in the year 1785, wrote:

Between twenty and thirty divorces are now granted annually by the superior court of Connecticut beside those given by the General Assembly. The desertion law is liberally construed.

In comparison with Connecticut there are but few divorces in any other parts of America. To whom then can we be likened for this great wickedness of putting away? Will even Pagan Rome present us with an equal? No, with respect to this, for the term of five, six or seven hundred years she stands forth as an uncontaminated virgin. During this long period she had not once done that which every year in numerous instances is perpetrated in Connecticut.

Is it not then time to stop and consider? High time unitedly to attempt a reformation? If matters are suffered to run on in their present channel, shall we not soon become like the nations of the world before the giving of the law when marriages were only for moons or years as suited the party? Or will it not be as it was in Rome after divorces grew into fashion, that married people will separate at pleasure.[6]

[6] Trumbull, *Unlawfulness of Divorce, an Appeal to the Public* (New Haven, 1788), Appendix.

28 STATISTICAL ANALYSIS OF AMERICAN DIVORCE

CHART 4

MAP OF STATES WITH DECREASING DIVORCE RATES SHOWN IN WHITE, 1929

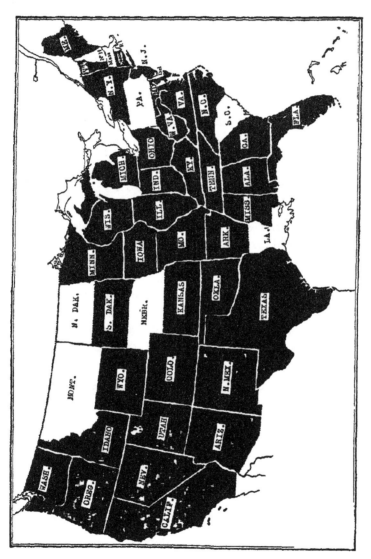

PROBABILITY OF DIVORCE

In spite of a divorce rate in the United States today, ten times the divorce rate of Connecticut at the end of the eighteenth century, the nation has not yet followed the Reverend Dr. Trumbull's pessimistic forecast of a collapse similar to the Roman Empire.

In 1891 Dr. Walter F. Willcox of Cornell University hazarded a prediction of the probability of American divorce in the future decades, as follows.

On the assumption that the conditions of the past twenty years, 1867-1886, remain unchanged and the population continues to increase through the next century at the rate of 28 per cent a decade and divorces at the rate of 69 per cent, the latter will constitute a rapidly increasing percentage of marriage dissolutions.[7]

Since all marriages are eventually ended by death or divorce, Dr. Willcox computed that for the year 1870, 3.5 per cent were dissolved by divorce and 96.5 were ended by death; 1880 showed 4.8 dissolution by divorce; and 1890, 6.2 per cent. On the assumption that the death rate would remain stationary and the divorce rate increase at the same ratio, Dr. Willcox in 1891 prognosticated that divorce would dissolve the following percentages of the total number of marriages.

TABLE 2   DECENNIAL ESTIMATES OF DIVORCE FREQUENCY

Year	Per cent	Year	Per cent
1900 –	8.0	1950 –	25.1
1910 –	10 4	1960 –	31.8
1920 –	13.3	1970 –	38.2
1930 –	16.8	1980 –	44.9
1940 –	21.0	1990 –	52.1
		2000 –	58 8

Professor Willcox added in modest explanation:

[7] Willcox, *The Divorce Problem, A Study in Statistics*, p. 20.

30 STATISTICAL ANALYSIS OF AMERICAN DIVORCE

It may be urged that the conditions will not be constant; that in fact they are rapidly altering, and it must be admitted that the population will not continue to increase at the rate of 28 per cent each decade, but thus far the progress of divorce has suffered no check.

It is not plain that such a computation has much value as determining the future. The elements are too varying and ill-determined to give good basis for a prediction. Such a calculation, however, has its importance as magnifying some ten diameters the past increase and making the meaning of the rate more obvious.[8]

It is unbelievable that Professor Willcox in 1891 forecast the United States divorce frequency for the year 1930, just about correctly.

Since a refined estimate (to be explained later) reveals that 18 per cent of American marriages end in divorce, as based on probabilities computed for the year 1928, at what future year will the majority of American marriages terminate in divorce? As previously shown, the divorce rate has uniformly increased. For the recent period, from the years 1922 to 1929, the divorce rate has compounded at a ratio of about 3 per cent annually. If this speed of advance continues, the year 1965, just thirty-three years from the present writing, would show about 51 per cent of American marriages ending in divorce. The adult death rate has not changed much in recent years. Even so, to project the past divorce rate of the United States into the future is merely a guess. In Chart 5, " Century Race Between Death and Divorce," divorce represents a growing space in black on the picture. The solid portion shows the increase for the past, while the cross-hatched area prognosticates the future role of divorce, contrasted to death in American family dissolution. The crucial matter will be to ascertain whether there

---

[8] Willcox, *The Divorce Problem, A Study in Statistics*, p. 20.

PROBABILITY OF DIVORCE

is a slackening in the activity of the factors that have caused an increase in the American divorce rate of more than 500 per cent from the Civil War to the present time.

CHART 5

CENTURY RACE BETWEEN DEATH AND DIVORCE

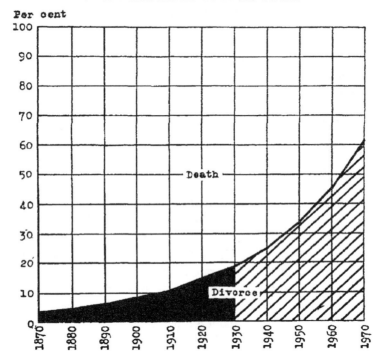

CHAPTER III

GROUNDS FOR DIVORCE

LEGAL causes for divorce are decided by legislative enactments in the states. Divorce applicants thus must fit their grievances to whatever grounds the statutes permit. The differences in the divorce laws of states offer slight explanation for the wide variations in divorce rates between the eastern and western districts of the country.

This is not an opportune place in the study to attempt to account for the higher divorce rates in the more newly settled regions of the United States A complexity of economic and social factors is probably responsible for the rise of divorce in almost all parts of the nation. The inhabitants of the West have been particularly subject to the intensity of environmental changes.

Chart 6 presents a sectional map of the country indicating high, medium and low divorce rates in the United States by geographical districts. As stated heretofore, the Pacific Coast states have three times the rate of the Atlantic Seaboard while the central states both north and south are intermediate in their divorce rates between these two extremes.

The following suggestions are from the *U. S. Marriage and Divorce Report* for 1928:

The wide variations in divorce rates among the different states doubtless result from a great variety of influences. Among these are differences in the color or race composition of the population; differences in the proportion of foreign-born in the population, and in the countries from which they came; the relative strength of prevailing religions, particularly the strength

32

GROUNDS FOR DIVORCE 33

CHART 6

MAP SHOWING PREVALENCE OF DIVORCE IN NINE GEOGRAPHICAL
SECTIONS OF THE COUNTRY, 1929

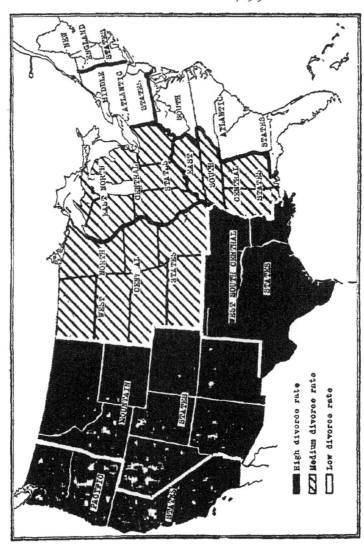

34 STATISTICAL ANALYSIS OF AMERICAN DIVORCE

of the Roman Catholic faith; interstate migration for the purpose of obtaining divorces; and variations in divorce laws and
in the practice of courts granting divorces.

Excluding states having only a few legal causes for divorce,
neither the difference between them in the number of legal
causes for divorce nor the difference of the kind or in the statement of these causes affords a complete explanation of existing
variation between states in the divorce rate or in the percentage
distribution by cause.[1]

Chart 7 likewise shows divorce rates according to the
nine census divisions of the country. Obviously the divorce
rate rises as one progresses westward.

CHART 7

COMPARATIVE DIVORCE RATES FOR THE NINE CENSUS DIVISIONS
OF THE NATION, 1929

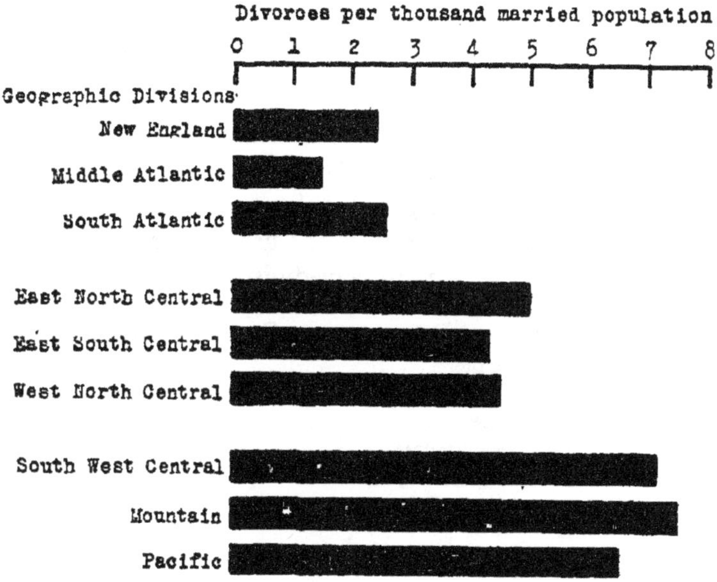

Divorces per thousand married population

Geographic Divisions:
- New England
- Middle Atlantic
- South Atlantic
- East North Central
- East South Central
- West North Central
- South West Central
- Mountain
- Pacific

[1] *U. S. Marriage and Divorce Report*, 1928, p. 16.

GROUNDS FOR DIVORCE

This preliminary presentation of the geographical distribution of divorce rates leads to the examination of the state legal grounds for divorce, which reveal or conceal underlying causes. The percentages indicating the leading grounds of divorce such as adultery, cruelty, desertion and so forth are contrasted for the earliest year recorded in American divorce statistics, 1867, with the recent data of 1928.

Dr. Carroll D. Wright, editor of the first government report, wrote the following explanation on this subject:

The deep underlying causes of divorce other than those stated in the libel or as found to exist by divorce courts, as for instance, industrial and sexual conditions, intemperance other than stated as a direct cause—in fact, all the social causes of divorce that lie beneath the exhibit of statistics, would have furnished material for a very close analysis and perhaps the complete analysis of divorce problems; but the impossibility of obtaining such information must be apparent upon the statement of their nature.[2]

The large circle in Chart 8 shows the distribution of divorces by principal legal grounds for the 10,000 cases granted in the year 1867. The item listed as combination causes in the report, meaning more than one ground for divorce, has been rearranged for a more refined distribution.

TABLE 3.   PERCENTAGE DISTRIBUTION OF GROUNDS OF DIVORCE, 1867

Adultery 33
Cruelty 13
Desertion 41
Drunkenness 3
Neglect to provide 2
Minor Grounds 8
_____
Total 100

[2] *U. S. Marriage and Divorce Report*, 1867-1886, p. 16.

CHART 8

Distribution of Grounds for Divorce, 1867

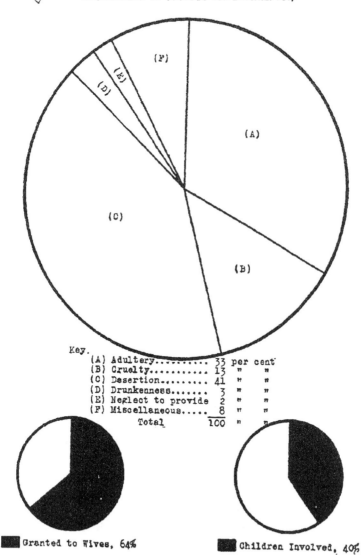

Key.
(A) Adultery.......... 33 per cent
(B) Cruelty.......... 13 " "
(C) Desertion........ 41 " "
(D) Drunkenness...... 3 " "
(E) Neglect to provide 2 " "
(F) Miscellaneous.... 8 " "
Total 100 " "

Granted to Wives, 64%

Children Involved, 40%

GROUNDS FOR DIVORCE

37

Chart 9 presents the percentage of divorces granted on various legal grounds, after reclassification, for the year 1928. The table following presents this distribution of divorces in suits where the husband was plaintiff, also suits where the wife was the complainant, and a combined average of both for 1928.

TABLE 4. PERCENTAGE DISTRIBUTION OF GROUNDS OF DIVORCE FOR HUSBAND AND WIFE, 1928

	Combined	Husband	Wife
Adultery	9	14	7
Cruelty	47	38	56
Desertion	32	45	26
Drunkenness	2	0	2
Neglect to provide	7	0	6
Minor grounds	3	3	3
Total	100	100	100

The principal changes in the distribution of divorces by grounds, in comparisons of 1867 and 1928, are for adultery and cruelty. Adultery is only one-fourth so frequent today while cruelty is employed four times as often, relatively, as a ground for divorce. This does not denote that the present era is four times as cruel and only one-fouth so unfaithful to the marriage vows, comparatively speaking, as was the period three generations ago. The increasing leniency of the courts in interpreting mental cruelty no longer makes it necessary for any considerable proportion of couples to bear the shameful publicity of a divorce trial on infidelity. This change in percentage of applications for divorce has not been due to modification of laws. The increasing laxity of judicial interpretations of cruelty as a ground for divorce is probably the result of a breakdown in social taboos against divorce, a change in the public mores due to the increasing number of divorced people within communities. Such attitudes develop from cumulative processes.

CHART 9

DISTRIBUTION OF GROUNDS FOR DIVORCE, 1928

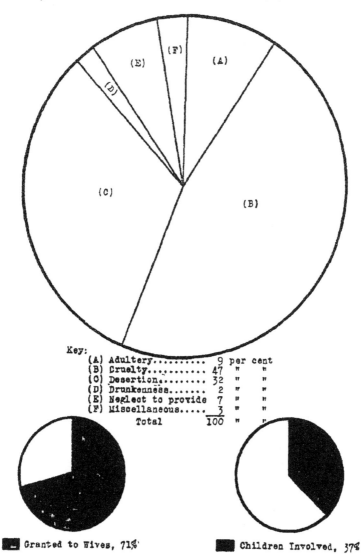

Key:
(A) Adultery........... 9 per cent
(B) Cruelty........... 47 " "
(C) Desertion......... 32 " "
(D) Drunkenness....... 2 " "
(E) Neglect to provide 7 " "
(F) Miscellaneous..... 3 " "
Total 100 " "

Granted to Wives, 71%

Children Involved, 37%

GROUNDS FOR DIVORCE

39

The difference of distributions in divorces granted to husbands and to wives, respectively, is not significant. The fact that the percentage of divorces granted to husbands on the ground of adultery was twice that granted to wives means nothing. The absolute numbers show that more divorces were given to women against adulterous husbands than were decreed to men from unfaithful wives. Cruelty is offered more frequently by the woman than the man, because it is an easy ground for a wife to prove. For a similar reason the husband employs desertion more frequently. It is obvious that divorces on the ground of neglect to provide must be granted to the wife since Utah is the only state which legalizes a male divorce for non-support. Drunkenness is likewise far more frequent among men than women.

The actual inaccuracies of these grounds for divorce are stated succinctly in the 1928 government report:

The statistics relating to the cause of divorce are based upon the legal causes as ascertained from court records. The legal cause shown by the court records may or may not, of course, be the true cause underlying the action for divorce When the husband and the wife both desire the divorce, it is probable that frequently the real cause for the action is not the cause alleged in the petition for divorce. Frequently too, the actual cause is not a legal cause in the particular state in which the court action takes place. For instance, neglect to provide is not listed as a cause for divorce in all states. In some jurisdictions suits brought primarily for this reason are granted on the grounds of cruelty; in others desertion is charged; gross neglect of duty is given as the cause in at least three; while in others, the husband is declared a vagrant in the eyes of the law, and the decree granted on the ground of vagrancy. For this reason it may truthfully be said that in a compilation of statistics covering divorce there is no phase of the subject so unsatisfactory to those interested in the study as the causes assigned for the granting of the decrees.[3]

[3] U. S. Marriage and Divorce Report, 1928, p. 22.

40   STATISTICAL ANALYSIS OF AMERICAN DIVORCE

For example, adultery is the ground for only three-tenths of one per cent of the divorces in Nevada, but is the ground for 59 per cent in North Carolina. Cruelty constitutes two-tenths of one per cent in Virginia, while 70 per cent of the Michigan divorces are on that ground. Drunkenness contributes 11 per cent in Illinois, while it is close to zero in other states allowing that same ground. Desertion is the ground for 5 per cent of divorces in Louisana, and 93 per cent in New Mexico. Rhode Island grants 63 per cent of its divorces to women for neglect to provide, and Utah 56 per cent. Divorce rates for various grounds fluctuate almost from zero to 100 per cent in the different states, and it is obvious that the American people are not ten times more cruel, adulterous or vagrant in some states than in others.

An attempt to glean the real causes of divorce from statistics regarding the grounds for divorce for the year 1928 is not very illuminating. Grounds for divorce seem to be employed interchangeably according to the wishes of the applicants. In the early years of marriage, cruelty and adultery occur most frequently. Neglect to provide happens most often in the middle years of life. If one passes these obstacles, desertion and drunkeness loom ahead, for both increase with the duration of marriage.

The crux of the matter concerning legal grounds is that virtually all states in the country allow divorces for cruelty and desertion. Cruelty is generally granted to wives and desertion to husbands. If the cruelty rate in the state is very high, the desertion rate is low, and vice versa. Obviously these two grounds, alleged for more than three-fourths of all divorces, are so flexible that they can vary from state to state for husband and wife without affecting the quota of divorces. Perhaps there exists some common, underlying source of divorce, regardless of whether it be stated as

GROUNDS FOR DIVORCE

41

cruelty or desertion in order to suit the laws of the state and to benefit parties by mutual consent. For further analysis the 1928 refined classification of the distribution of grounds for divorce is resubmitted.

TABLE 5. REFINED CLASSIFICATION OF GROUNDS OF DIVORCE ON PERCENTAGE BASIS, 1928

Adultery	9
Cruelty	47
Desertion	32
Drunkenness	2
Neglect to provide	7
Minor grounds	3
Total	100

The table shows that 79 per cent of the divorces were granted on the more or less anomalous charges of cruelty and desertion. However, one must refine this rate in order to secure greater accuracy. Some legal desertions are actually long separations of many years and are bona-fide desertions. The Louisiana figures are the only ones available on this score.[4] Divorce in that state is granted, only on adultery or seven years' desertion. Nevertheless, about 16 per cent of the divorces are granted for desertion, and since Louisiana's divorce rate is about one-half that of the country, one may conclude that about 8 per cent of divorces are bona-fide desertions; 32 per cent is the figure listed in the table. It is useless, however, to try to analyze the 47 per cent cruelty figures because almost all judges have observed that divorces occurring under this ground are not of the strictly necessitous type. Neglect to provide cannot be called a severe cause for breaking the marriage vow. That leaves adultery with 9 per cent, drunkenness—2 per

[4] The assumption of typicality in this instance of Louisiana is due to the small percentages of divorces on desertion in other states where the statute demands several years of separation.

42   STATISTICAL ANALYSIS OF AMERICAN DIVORCE

cent, and the minor grounds—3 per cent (these evidently are rather serious, such as felony, insanity and bigamy). However, the aforementioned group does not constitute the only valid grounds for divorces. It is a difficult problem to divide divorces into one class where marriages are dissolved due to grave causes and another group based simply upon mutual incompatibility

There probably are other valid divorces beside the 14 per cent listed under adultery, drunkenness, felony, insanity, bigamy and so forth, plus an added 8 per cent due to long-time desertions   The 9 per cent for adultery must be considerably under-estimated, with a consequent exaggeration of the cruelty and desertion figures.   As a ground for divorce adultery is negligible in the Far West and very frequent in the East.   This is probably not due to a difference in human nature in these two sections of the country but merely to the difference in laws.   New York, the District of Columbia, North Carolina and Louisiana have such strict laws that practically all their divorces are granted upon adultery.   However, the number of divorces on infidelity in these four states with respect to their populations constitutes a divorce rate only one-fifth the national rate, or about 20 per cent.   Obviously divorce applicants are required to make the adultery charge in those states where no other recourse is open to them.   However, this indicates that if such laws existed in all states, the divorce rate would drop about 80 per cent for the country.[5]   The conclusion is that about 20 per cent of divorces are due to adultery instead of 9 per cent. The 9 per cent figure exists merely because it is easier to charge cruelty or even desertion in liberal jurisdictions.

Since probably one-fifth of the divorces are directly due to infidelity, a consequent reduction would have to be made in the percentage for cruelty which was previously classified

[5] The relevant situation here of migratory divorce is examined in ch. v.

GROUNDS FOR DIVORCE

43

under mutual incompatibility, because some of the 47 per cent listed as cruelty charges are hiding infidelity. Concerning the valid grounds for divorce in the strict sense of the word one can now include adultery with 20 per cent, drunkenness 2 per cent, minor grounds 3 per cent and long-time desertions 8 per cent, summing approximately 33 per cent, or about one-third of the total divorces. The remaining two-thirds are listed under cruelty, desertion and neglect to provide. These are uncontested usually and predominate in the liberal western divorce regions of America. They represent that big failing in marital life which judges call mutual incompatibility.

Further substantiation of this idea is the small number of contested divorce suits, amounting to only 12 per cent of the total. The majority of these contests are probably of a technical nature concerning matters such as the disposition of children, alimony or the jurisdiction of the court, and are not genuine attempts to prevent the divorce. This overwhelming prevalence of mutual consent in American divorce is not revealed by such blanket, legal terms as cruelty or desertion.

Dr. Ernest R. Mowrer of Northwestern University says:

The establishment of a family is the process of building up organized attitudes in which all concur. Family disorganization represents a converse process in which the family complex breaks up and the ambitions and ideals of the individual members of the family become differentiated.

The legal aspects of marriage and divorce are recognition by the community or state that family attitudes have been established or are disintegrated.[6]

Apropos of the changing American attitude toward divorce, stressing mutual incompatibility, an editorial in

[6] Mowrer, *Family Disorganization* (Chicago, 1927), p. 4.

44 STATISTICAL ANALYSIS OF AMERICAN DIVORCE

World's Work reads: " In marriage, partnership has given way to a sort of limited liability stock corporation in which husband and wife buy shares at the altar with a tacit understanding that at any later date either may sell out his interest and retire from the business." [7]

The analysis of alleged legal grounds for divorce demonstrates their unreliability as causal explanations of this problem. About one-third of the divorces are classified as due to grave causes, while the remaining two-thirds consist of the mutual incompatibility type. The chapter is preparatory to an investigation of real influences effecting American family breakdown.

[7] *World's Work*, December, 1926, p. 125.

CHAPTER IV

Underlying Conditions

What are the underlying conditions that motivate divorces? What are the true causes which drive about 200,000 American families in a single year to resort to the divorce courts for freedom from marital ties? If these basic causes could be discovered, then perhaps they would explain the fundamental changes in the trend of the American divorce rate in its rapid advance during the past sixty-three years.

The chapter consists of a symposium of opinions on the causes of divorce taken from a journalistic survey of views of judges and psychiatrists, a personal interview with a noted judge, and the detailed analysis given by a prominent sociologist. Then some divers hypotheses are tested with the aid of statistical methods. This study is concerned primarily with causes of increasing divorce during the last six decades, so that this chapter on the contemporary causes of marital discord is introductory to the main issue.

The Reverend Rollin L. Hartt made a survey of the leading American divorce courts, a study called "The Habit of Getting Divorces." [1] The Reverend Mr. Hartt interviewed the leading judges and domestic relations experts throughout the country. The wide variations in opinion of these authorities show the striking divergence of views and solutions for this complex problem.

Dr. William J. Hickson, psychiatrist of the Chicago Court of Domestic Relations, believed the principal causes of divorce to be the following:

[1] Hartt, "The Habit of Getting Divorces," *Worlds Work*, August, 1924, pp. 403-409.

46 STATISTICAL ANALYSIS OF AMERICAN DIVORCE

(1) Feeblemindedness plus dementia praecox.
(2) Dementia praecox.
(3) Feeblemindedness.

Dr. Hickson said that all economic classes of people were susceptible to divorce. He further stated that a big asylum committing two thousand insane and feebleminded patients annually, recruited its inmates solely from the Chicago Court of Domestic Relations.

In the same building Judge William L. Morgan gave very different reasons as the fundamental causes of divorce. Judge Morgan believes that divorces are more frequent among the lower economic strata of society. His list of causes follows:

(1) Poverty.
(2) Neglect of women by husbands.
(3) Low mentality.
(4) Drink.
(5) Nagging.
(6) Improper sex mating.

Judge C. W. Hoffman of the Cincinnati Court of Domestic Relations has obtained the aid of social workers and psychiatrists in diagnosing the causes of divorce. Judge Hoffman believes from confidential court confessions that nine out of ten divorce cases are due to the sexual degeneracy of the husband. He further states that the court complaints are merely light talk, because at least three-fourths of the divorcees had valid grounds but would perjure themselves rather than speak the facts in court. He thinks that divorces are more common among the poorer classes.

Attorney Leonard McGee, Chief of the Legal Aid Society of New York, handled four thousand domestic difficulty cases a year from 1920 to 1925. Ninety-five per cent of these cases were settled without litigation. Attorney McGee, -

UNDERLYING CONDITIONS

who has since become a judge, believes there is no single outstanding cause of divorce. When questioned by the Reverend Mr. Hartt, he would not agree to any of the singular interpretations of divorce given by certain judges.

Dr. Katherine B. Davis, General Secretary of the Bureau of Social Hygiene in New York City, thinks that physical mismating is the overwhelming cause of divorce. This opinion was formulated from replies of questionnaires to several thousand married women mostly of the wealthy and educated classes.

The Reverend Dr. John G. Benson presides over the social clinic of a west forty-eighth street Methodist church in New York, which investigates 14,000 domestic relations cases annually. He believes that in 80 per cent of the disputes the woman wishes to save the home. He gives as a list of principal causes of divorce the following:

(1) Adultery.
(2) Relatives.
(3) Physical incompatibility.
(4) Female independence.

The Reverend Ralph H. Ferris, a former professor in Chicago Theological Seminary and a major in the World War, directs the Bureau of Domestic Relations in Detroit. He has dealt with cases of 20,000 couples. His list of principal causes follows:

(1) Hasty marriages on physical attraction—quarrels when economic pinch occurs.
(2) Lack of religion—majority not church attendants, even though they belong.
(3) Drink.
(4) Uncontrolled temper.

Major Ferris adds, " Most of the divorcees are subnormal, borderline semi-criminal types, mostly registered at hos-

48   STATISTICAL ANALYSIS OF AMERICAN DIVORCE

pitals and social agencies.   They are physically, economically and socially inadequate and, therefore, failures."

Judge Bradley Hull of Cleveland was for four years Director of the Bureau of Domestic Relations in Cleveland. He distinctly does not believe in the psychopathic elements alleged as causes of divorce.   His own interpretations are as follows:

(1) Economic pinch, primarily.

(2) Nerves.

(3) Faulty education.

In conclusion, the Reverend Mr. Hartt notes that the various experts contradict each other in emphasizing causes. Of eight distinguished investigators no two reached identical conclusions as to the principal causes of divorce.

Judges all over the country admit that underlying causes are deliberately concealed in court statements.   Very few divorces are refused anywhere according to the consensus of judges.   The variety of causes afforded by these different psychiatrists and judges, as well as their conflicting opinions, indicates that there is no single interpretation of this complex question in social metabolism known as family breakdown. All together these experts stated twenty separate causes of divorce.

For a more intimate view of this human problem, the author attended the trials of some divorce cases in Judge Joseph Sabath's Chicago divorce court.   Sessions at this tribunal, which probably handles more domestic relations cases than any other in the world, are more interesting than enlightening, due to the doubtful truth of statements by complainants.

In the great majority of cases the wife sues for divorce. Most of these marriages about to be dissolved bore no children.   There is usually no contest, the husband not even appearing in court.   Alimony settlements are infrequent.

UNDERLYING CONDITIONS

49

A wife accuses her husband of cruelty or desertion or drunkenness, or perhaps a combination of these. Her statements are prepared and automatic in answer to the expected questions of her attorney. One or two witnesses follow, and swear to the truth of the plaintiff's statements. They cite instances of cruelty, such as a swear word, a slap in the face or a broken promise to return home on a certain evening. Only the judge, the attorney and the newspaper reporters are able to hear these statements. The court room, however, is crowded with spectators. They are plaintiffs and witnesses waiting their turn to appear at the tribunal of justice where the ties of matrimony are dissolved. Divorce cases of this type average about a dozen an hour in a Chicago court.

There are exceptional cases which take much longer, such as contested divorce suits or those where a problem over the disposition of children arises. Then Judge Sabath often requires long and detailed hearings of the facts of the case, and tries his best to reconcile the parties and preserve the home.

Judge Sabath was kind enough to grant an interview to query his opinions and experiences on divorce. He believes that poverty applies in the largest percentage of divorce cases, separating more families than any other individual cause. He does not think divorcees belong to subnormal types. His opinion is that mutual incompatibility is of outstanding importance caused by temperamental mismating. Judge Sabath does not think incompatible persons can be forced to live together. Their difficulty, he believes, often commences as tiny affairs, such irritations and disagreements constantly accumulating until the couple have separated. This can be termed temperamental incompatibility. Finally Judge Sabath adds that divorces are within the price of all. Costs are moderate upon a graduated scale according to income. Judge Sabath deservedly has a great humanitarian reputa-

50   STATISTICAL ANALYSIS OF AMERICAN DIVORCE

tion, for in eight years he has actually reunited more than 2,500 couples after bills of divorce had been filed.

Professor Ogburn takes a different approach to the problem of family disintegration, but his conclusions are not significantly different from previously stated opinions.[2]   His method is a classification of the functions of the family, with statistical evidence to show their various declines.   First, the affectional function has been weakened by desertion and infidelity.

Second, the economic function of the home is undergoing vast changes as indicated by the rapid increases of restaurants, waiters, bakeries, delicatessens, canning and preserving employees and laundries.   Statistical evidence which he presents indicates that the afore-mentioned factors are depriving the home of the traditional duties of the housewife. Moreover, sewing machines have declined in number indicating another loss of the home function of women.   Regarding the increased number of female wage-earners, Dr. Ogburn writes:

These statistics of married women working for pay are the dramatic testimony of the changing status of the home.   The movement is swift and still continues. . . . Another possible index of the declining economic functions of the family is the increase in the number of multi-family dwellings.   Such flats or apartments are usually smaller than houses without yards or much play space.   Quite generally, the heating is done by some one other than a member of the family.   They are, therefore, a symbol of fewer household duties in the United States.[3]

There has been a rapid increase in the issuance of this type of building permit.

Third, the educational function of the family has declined, due both to the increasing percentage of children who attend

---

[2] Ogburn, "The Changing Family," *Publications of the American Sociological Society*, October, 1929, pp. 124-133.

[3] *Ibid*, p. 129.

UNDERLYING CONDITIONS

school for a longer number of years and a greater part of the year than formerly, and also to the declining number of children in the family.

Fourth, the recreational function of the family formerly was centered in the home. The vast increase in moving picture shows, parks and playgrounds has provided a strong substitute.

Fifth, the protective function of the family has to a large extent been replaced by the state as indicated by the large increases in the number of policemen, guards, watchmen, officials and inspectors, as well as the advances in child labor laws, compulsory education laws and social insurance.

Professor Ogburn summarizes these changes:

Statistical evidence shows that the family is declining in regard to the number of functions it performs, and that the affectional function is not performed satisfactorily in many cases. Broken families are frequent. The economic function has declined markedly. The recreational and protectional functions are small. So also is the educational function. This movement is operating strongly at the present time with few signs of slackening.[4]

The foregoing summary of opinions on the causes of divorce is a condensation of the Reverend Mr. Hartt's symposium of judges and psychiatrists, personal attendance at Judge Sabath's Chicago court of domestic relations, and Professor Ogburn's functional analysis of family disintegration. The causes of divorce listed by these authorities will be liberally classified into the following five general categories; degeneracy, poverty, religious decline, urbanization and woman's freedom.

[4] Ogburn, "The Changing Family," *Publications of the American Sociological Society*, October, 1929, p. 133.

52 STATISTICAL ANALYSIS OF AMERICAN DIVORCE

CHART 10

STANDARD AREA DIVORCE MAP OF THIRTY-NINE STATES, 1929

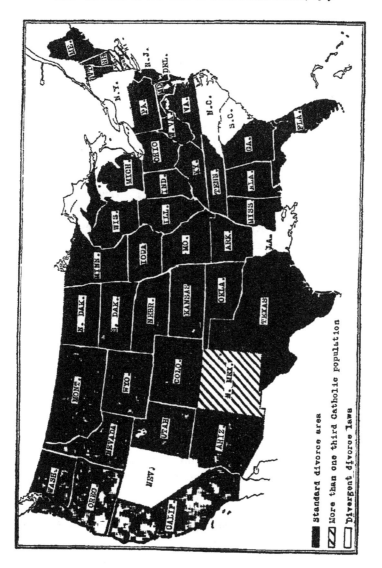

UNDERLYING CONDITIONS   53

These causes will now be elaborated as hypotheses and tested by their conformity to statistical data. For correlation purposes, the divorce rates of the states constitute the dependent variable, while certain economic and vital indices are the independent variables. There are forty-nine divorce jurisdictions in the United States, but ten are omitted from correlation set-ups due to their peculiar divorce laws or religious composition. The standard area map, Chart 10, depicts in black the 39 states that have fairly uniform laws and therefore are selected for correlation purposes. South Carolina could not be included because it bars divorce; Nevada is too lax in its residence requirements; District of Columbia, Louisiana, New York and North Carolina are legally very stringent; Connecticut, Massachusetts, New Mexico and Rhode Island consist of populations more than one-third of whom follow the Roman Catholic religion. These ten states were omitted because the correlation of divorce rates of states with economic and social indices demands that legal and religious factors be lessened in influence as much as possible.

The previously stated opinions of psychiatrists and some judges signify the principal cause of divorce to be degeneracy, including such sinister features as crime, disease, feeble-mindedness, immorality, insanity and sexual maladjustments. It must be remembered that judges and psychiatrists see the most gloomy aspects in the problems of family disruption, and therefore are prejudiced somewhat toward a morbid interpretation of divorce. Careful scrutiny of the facts from the standpoint of the entire country is required to ascertain whether degeneracy is the prime cause of divorce. First, since divorce is three times as frequent on the Pacific Coast as on the Atlantic Seaboard, is it credible that the Far Westerners are thrice as degenerate as Eastern Americans? Second, a correlation by states between divorce rates for 1929 and illegitimacy resulted in a coefficient —.29.[5] This

[5] *U. S. Birth, Stillbirth and Infant Mortality Statistics*, 1928, pp. 12-13.

54 STATISTICAL ANALYSIS OF AMERICAN DIVORCE

coefficient is small in size, and indicates that no positive association will probably be found between divorce and illegitimacy, further discrediting the degeneracy notion of divorce. Third, the chief evidence against such a sinister view of the divorce problem is that about one-half the divorces occur after seven years of marriage. Certainly if physical incompatibility and mental abnormality were so prevalent in marriages that eventually end in divorce, such marriages would probably collapse within a year after the ceremony. Perhaps an additional year should be allowed in many cases to provide for court delays. The facts show that only twelve per cent of the total divorces from all causes occur during the first two years of marriage, thus substantially undermining the degeneracy explanation of divorce.

That poverty is a frequent accompaniment of divorce was prominent in the opinions of practically all the judges. Again it must be recalled the vast majority of people in metropolitan cities, both in and outside divorce courts, belong to comparatively poor classes or to those groups which do not pay income taxes. Moreover, since judges see many divorce applicants in periods of severe misery, their natural inclinations are to ascribe indigence to these distressed people. The first refutation of this idea is that increasing poverty could not account for the fivefold advance in the divorce rate during the last six decades, because the American standards of living have admittedly risen since 1870. Second, a correlation between divorce rates and an economic index of well-being fails to indicate that poverty is positively associated with divorce. Due to lack of a more suitable economic series, automobile registration was chosen to represent the standard of living; and a correlation between 1929 divorce rates and automobiles per hundred population figures for 39 states gave a negligible coefficient +.18.[6] This coefficient

[6] U. S. Statistical Abstract, 1930, p. 388.

UNDERLYING CONDITIONS

is too small in size to be significant, but at least the association is not negative, which would be required to stress the dependence of divorce on poverty. Professor Ogburn correlated divorced persons of 170 American cities with the respective amounts of manufacturing, a partial correlation holding two other factors constant, giving a coefficient —.36 [7] Dr. Ogburn admits this result is surprising, since manufacturing would not be expected to curtail divorce rates; but here legal and religious factors interfere, as many of these cities are in New York where the law is strict or in New England where high percentages of the people are Catholic. It is generally agreed that cities with the greater degree of manufacturing would also be those where poverty is more severe. The partial correlation coefficient —.36 indicates a moderate degree of negative association between manufacturing and divorce. All of the foregoing facts and correlations fail to indicate a positive association between divorce and poverty.

Religious decline is listed by several of the previously quoted experts as an important cause of divorce. Ecclesiastical legislation in America concerning divorce must first be surveyed, and it approximates the following:

The Roman Catholic Church forbids divorce.

The Protestant Episcopal Church permits divorce for adultery and desertion.

The Congregational Church allows divorce for adultery.

The Reformed Church permits divorce for adultery.

The Presbyterian Church allows divorce for adultery.

The Methodist Episcopal Church permits divorce for adultery and desertion.

The Evangelical Lutheran Church allows divorce for adultery and desertion.

[7] Groves and Ogburn, *American Marriage and Family Relationships*, p. 375.

56 *STATISTICAL ANALYSIS OF AMERICAN DIVORCE*

Ecclesiastical changes have been few and slow.[8] In 1928 the Methodist Episcopal Church liberalized its divorce code by permitting ministers to remarry persons who had been divorced on the ground of desertion. Previously only adultery had been tolerated. In the year 1930 the United Lutheran Church restricted its divorce laws by repealing the ecclesiastical regulation which had previously permitted divorce upon the ground of extreme cruelty. In 1931, the Presbyterians restricted divorce by abolishing desertion as a rightful cause.

Professor James P Lichtenberger of the University of Pennsylvania, after admission of the very low divorce rates among Catholics, summarized the activities of the Protestant Churches as follows: " With the growing frequency of divorce the churches have been increasingly active on this subject and there has been a constant tendency toward stringency in ecclesiastical matters. The churches have sought to oppose the tendencies revealed in the rising divorce rate by increasing the strength of ecclesiastical control." [9]

That divorce rates are substantially lower in districts in the United States where Catholics predominate is generally admitted. A correlation between divorce rates for 1929 with Catholicism included 43 states, Connecticut, Massachusetts, New Mexico and Rhode Island being added to the standard area.[10] The value of the coefficient —.45 indicates a moderate association between low divorce rates and Catholicism.

[8] The most recent modification was enacted by the National Episcopal Church at its Denver Conference in September, 1931. The divorce canon was very slightly relaxed to permit the remarriage of the innocent party in a divorce on adultery, provided that the bishop of the diocese annuls the prior marriage.

[9] Lichtenberger, *Divorce a Study in Social Causation* (New York, 1909), p. 141.

[10] *U. S. Census, Religious Bodies,* 1926 (Washington, 1929), vol. ii, p. 1256.

UNDERLYING CONDITIONS

Since only one-sixth of the American population is Catholic, divorce, so far as it is a religious problem, is primarily concerned with Protestant believers. Cruelty is the most frequently employed legal ground for divorce, being the alleged judicial cause of almost half of the American divorces. However, cruelty is not tolerated as a ground for divorce by any of the leading Protestant churches, thus showing a lessening influence of the church upon the conduct of some of its members.

On the other hand, church membership figures for the United States give no indication of religious decline. A 1926 enumeration shows that church membership in America increased about 19 per cent from 1906 to 1916, while population advanced 21 per cent; and from 1916 to 1926 church membership increased 18 per cent compared with a 15 per cent advance of population.[11] Therefore, church membership has augmented about as rapidly in this country as the population.

It is difficult to summarize this meager evidence under the heading of religious decline as a cause of divorce, especially since religious attitudes are to a large extent intangible. Admittedly Catholicism is a deterrent influence upon divorce in this country. The Protestant churches have not diminished in membership, nor has ecclesiastical legislation upon divorce been relaxed. On the other hand, the lessening spiritual influence of the church upon the conduct of its adherents is plainly shown by the fact that the majority of divorces today were granted on grounds other than adultery and desertion, which alone are tolerated by the churches.

Urbanization, or the increasing encroachment of city activity upon home life, is named as a cause of divorce by several of the previously quoted judges, and includes Professor Ogburn's economic, recreational and protective categories, that he lists as declining functions of the family.

[11] *U. S. Census, Religious Bodies,* 1926, vol. i, p. 48.

58   STATISTICAL ANALYSIS OF AMERICAN DIVORCE

The comparative divorce rates of city and country have been discussed for many decades.   The second *U. S. Marriage and Divorce Report,* published in 1908, listed comparative divorce rates for urban and rural counties in a considerable number of states for the decennial years 1870, 1880, 1890 and 1900.   The average for each period uniformly showed the city rates to be only about 10 per cent higher. However, the *U. S. Marriage and Divorce Report* for 1924 gave comparative divorce rates for the largest cities in the United States contrasted to the remainders of the population in their respective states during the year.   Baltimore, Boston Buffalo, Chicago, Cleveland, Denver, New Orleans, Norfolk, Philadelphia, Pittsburgh, Richmond, San Francisco and St. Louis all showed divorce rates above those of the rural sections of their states, the net average with little variation being about 50 per cent higher for these cities.   New York City alone was slightly below the state level due to its foreign population.

Professor Ogburn undertook a refined analysis of urban and rural divorce rates.   It is recognized that the difference between these would be greater if the foreign populations in municipalities did not tend to hold down the divorce rates there.   Dr. Ogburn's summary percentages of the population divorced for five selected states follow: [12]

TABLE 6   AVERAGE PERCENTAGES DIVORCED OF THE URBAN AND RURAL
RACIAL POPULATIONS OF THE FIVE SELECTED STATES, 1920

Racial and Nativity Groups	Urban	Rural
Native white of native parentage	1 12	.50
Foreign or mixed parentage	.87	.43
Foreign born	.53	.40
Negro	1 76	1.11

[12] These states are Illinois, Missouri, Ohio, Pennsylvania and Texas. Groves and Ogburn. *American Marriages and Family Relationships,* p. 373.

UNDERLYING CONDITIONS 59

Divorce rates are thus substantially higher in the urban population. The native-born white Americans have a much higher rate than the foreign-born, while those classified as foreign or mixed parentage fall midway between these two groups. The negro population in these five states has a divorce rate considerably higher than the native-born white.[13] It may be well to note here that about three-fourths of the American population by the 1920 census were native born white.[14]

An attempt is now made to analyze in detail the decennial figures for statistics of divorced persons as classified in the urban and rural distribution. The number of divorced persons reported in the 1920 decennial census is admittedly under-estimated, but there seems to be no reason why it should be relatively more or less accurate on the farms than in the cities. Such computations are not valid for divorced females. The number listed is so much smaller than divorced men in the rural districts that it must be deficient probably because rural women in many cases after being divorced move to the city to avoid social ostracism and to earn a living.

By computation of figures for the male population, the ratio of the number of all divorced men to the number of married men listed in the 1920 census was 1.08 per cent, the urban ratio was 1.23 per cent, the rural .91 per cent.[15] As previously stated the foreign population groups in cities, many of whom are Catholics, lower the divorce rates there; consequently the endeavor is made to obtain ratios based merely on the male population of native-born whites of native parentage for urban and rural districts. The ratio of all native-born white men of native parentage who were di-

[13] Groves and Ogburn, *American Marriage and Family Relationships*, p 373

[14] *U. S. Census*, 1920, vol. ii, p. 33.

[15] *U. S. Census*, 1920, vol. ii, p. 576.

60   STATISTICAL ANALYSIS OF AMERICAN DIVORCE

vorced to married men was 1.20 per cent. For the urban population this figure constituted 1.60 per cent. The rural population showed .89 per cent. These are about the most refined data available on the subject, and indicate that divorce rates in urban territory are almost double rural divorces rates.

A press release of the yet unpublished 1930 census confirms this estimate.[16] For the male population fifteen years old and over, 1.3 per cent of all persons living in communities of over 2,500 people were divorced, 1.2 per cent of men in communities under 2,500 inhabitants, while only .7 per cent of men living on farms were enumerated as divorced.

This evidence at first seems contradictory to the obvious facts that divorce rates are much higher in the agricultural states of the West than in the industrial states of the East. However, urbanization is only one of a number of factors affecting divorce This is a complex problem of social causation involving a number of interacting causes, so that no singular interpretation can be accepted. Reasons for divorce rates being higher in rural than urban states are the predominance of foreigners and Catholics in many cities near the Atlantic Seaboard and the stringent laws of New York and the District of Columbia. Furthermore, the large cities in Western states have consistently higher divorce rates than the neighboring agricultural regions as likewise do cities in the East. Thus when factors involving legislation, nationality and religion are held constant, urbanization appears to be a prominent cause of divorce.

Woman's freedom or the modern emancipation of the wife from dependence on the husband is asserted to be a leading cause of divorce by most of the judges. Their opinions are supported by the evidence that 71 per cent of all divorces at the present time are granted to wives. That the wife insti-

[16] *U. S. Census*, press release 7, Aug. 31, 1931.

UNDERLYING CONDITIONS 61

gates the suit in divorce court has always been preeminent in American family history. In 1867, when the divorce rate in the United States was only one-fifth its present size, wives were then granted 64 per cent of the total divorces.

Equal legal rights for wives in divorce courts are readily admitted, but it is more fundamental to ascertain the extent of woman's economic dependence on man. Professor Ogburn correlated divorced persons with employed women for 170 cities. A partial correlation holding two factors constant, gave a coefficient—.20.[17] Although the size of this coefficient is too small from which to derive conclusions, the surprising negative association between divorce and employed women can probably be ascribed to counteracting legal and religious factors involved in this correlation data, since many of the cities were in New York and New England.

On the other hand, evidence of woman's economic ability to earn a living is indirectly shown in the minor consequence of alimony in divorce proceedings. For the period of the first *U. S. Marriage and Divorce Report,* 1867-1886, only 16 per cent of the wives demanded alimony and 12 per cent received it. The 1887-1906 government report showed that 13 per cent asked for alimony and 9 per cent were granted it. For the latest available year only 9 per cent of the wives requested alimony and 6 per cent were given it.

Clear evidence as to the influence of woman's freedom as a cause of divorce is fragmentary, except that wives apply for 71 per cent of American divorces and the marked fact that only 6 per cent of divorced women receive alimony.

From the testimony of the preceding experts five hypotheses were set forth as to principal causes of divorce. These were tested for conformity with statistical data on the

[17] Groves and Ogburn, *American Marriage and Family Relationships,* p. 376.

62 STATISTICAL ANALYSIS OF AMERICAN DIVORCE

subject, and the results indicate that degeneracy and poverty are not leading causes of divorce, that evidence on religious decline and woman's freedom as causes of divorce is too uncertain to permit generalization, and that urbanization or the encroachment of city life upon the functions of the family appears to be distinctly associated with divorce.

Urbanization is closely interwoven with many other factors in family breakdown. The percentage of women workers is higher in cities than in rural districts, while the birthrate is lower in urban communities than in the country. Here are two vital indices representing the disintegration of the family, the economic independence of the wife and fewer children in the home, both these conditions being more prevalent in cities. Furthermore, urbanization is synonymous with growing economic production and the accelerated speed of living in industrial cities, such circumstances tending to cause increased friction in family circles. City life involves a complexity of interacting factors affecting the unity of the home, that are reflected later and to a lesser degree in the country, thus accounting for the consistently higher divorce rates of urban communities over rural districts within the same states.

This entire analysis has been concerned with objective causes of divorce, factors outside the home that have produced a weakening of the family bonds of cohesion. A changing economic and social environment creates many maladjustments in the family relationship leading to mutual incompatibility.

This last term is a symptom of the environmental factors conditioning divorce rather than a cause itself. Subjective forces in personal motives, that vital matter of the human equation, which impel people to seek divorces, are not within the scope of this investigation. Such inner causes are scarcely measurable by factual indices and perhaps are not clearly known even to the divorce applicants themselves.

CHAPTER V

MIGRATORY DIVORCE

MIGRATORY divorce, marriage and divorce legislation, and the desire for remarriage are three factors that are frequently supposed to be important causes of increasing divorces. Statistical evidence will be marshaled in this and the following two chapters to elicit the truth or falsity of these popular notions.

The subject of interstate migration for divorce is often a lively topic in public discussion. Do people cross state boundary lines in order to gain divorces in evasion of the laws of their own particular commonwealths? Migratory divorces must not be confused with what shall be termed for convenience, non-resident divorces. This country has a shifting population moving from state to state, so that large groups of people without any evasive purposes acquire non-resident divorces; that is, divorce in different states from those in which they were married. What percentage migrates solely to avoid the statutes in the home states?

After analysis of the figures for the 1867-1886 divorce survey, Dr. Dike, Executive Secretary of the National Divorce Reform League, wrote that migration from state to state for divorce under easier conditions must really constitute a small percentage of the great total, perhaps 3 per cent.[1] Before the figures had been published, he was under the impression that a vastly greater number of divorces was of the migratory nature.

[1] Dike, " Statistics of Marriage and Divorce," *Quarterly Publications of the American Statistical Association*, March, 1889, p. 212.

64   STATISTICAL ANALYSIS OF AMERICAN DIVORCE

This popular impression is very old. Already in 1856 an attorney from Michigan wrote in *Putnam's Magazine* as follows: " A mania has prevailed in our vicinity for Indiana divorces. The very perceptible increase of the profits of the Michigan Southern Railway may be directly traced to people rushing to Indiana for divorce." [2]   Dr. Wright, the editor of the first government report on divorce, later wrote: " The truth seems to be that the residence of a few notorious persons in states having lax divorce laws makes a greater impression on the public mind than is warranted by the facts." [3]

Professor Willcox has summarized this problem in his recent article on divorce in the *Encyclopedia Britannica:*

A frequent mistake made regarding divorce in the United States, which does not find warrant in the statistics on the subject, is that a very large proportion of divorces is granted to persons who move from one jurisdiction to another in order to avail themselves of lax divorce laws. Evidence is nearly conclusive, and has gone far towards decreasing the demand for a constitutional amendment allowing a federal marriage and divorce law   About four-fifths of all the divorces granted in the United States were issued to parties who were married in the state in which the decree of divorce was later made, and when from the remaining one-fifth are deducted those in which the parties migrated for other reasons than a desire to obtain an easy divorce, the remainder would be a very small almost a negligible fraction of the total number. [4]

Preliminary to the analysis of interstate divorce migration first will be considered the alleged evil of Americans obtaining divorces in Paris and Mexico. This notoriety is due to newspaper publicity given wealthy persons. Dr. Lindell T.

[2] *Putnam's Magazine*, December, 1856, p. 635.

[3] Wright, *Outline of Practical Sociology* (New York, 1909), p. 167.

[4] Willcox, " Divorce in the U. S.," *Encyclopedia Britannica* (London, 1929), vol. viii, p. 460.

MIGRATORY DIVORCE

Bates, an American attorney in France, has analyzed the subject of Parisian divorces.[5] He declares that before the war there were comparatively few American divorces in France. About one hundred occurred in 1922. This number steadily rose to about three hundred in 1926. Three months' residence only was required, and the secretiveness of the court hearing was attractive to Americans. However, American newspapers began to publish a list of divorces in 1927, and the French government demanded additionally a valid residence requirement. Thereupon a reaction set in. The price of divorce doubled, reaching at least $1500 and the number of divorces fell to less than two hundred in 1927. Most Parisian divorces have been granted to New Yorkers, but in the majority of cases where legal validity was tested, the New York courts refused to sanction these decrees. The number of divorces for Americans in Paris is still rapidly decreasing.

Another wealthy divorce resort is Mexico, where divorces are granted to Americans in about three days' time for $1500. Attorney Bates in another writing recently has carefully estimated that over two thousand divorces have been granted to Americans in Mexico since the War.[6] That would be about two hundred a year, mostly to New Yorkers. New York and other American state courts have consistently refused to uphold the legal validity of divorces granted in Mexico. However, the parties can remarry in Mexico, and not later be prosecuted for bigamy in the United States.

In recent months there has been an added impetus to Mexican divorces due to advertising pressure and the privilege of divorces by mail in some Mexican provinces. Also Havana, Cuba, has opened a divorce mill to cater to wealthy American patrons.

[5] Bates, *The Divorce and Separation of Aliens in France* (New York, 1929), ch. iii.

[6] Bates, *American Bar Association Journal*, November, 1929, pp. 709-713.

66   STATISTICAL ANALYSIS OF AMERICAN DIVORCE

When it is recalled that about 200,000 divorces are annually granted in the United States, then a few hundred divorces to Americans in Paris and Mexico constitute a negligible but noisy minority.

The U. S. Marriage and Divorce Report for 1922 was the latest to give the extent of interstate migration among divorced couples known to have been married in the United States. The statistics show that 26 per cent of those known to have been married in the United States were divorced in different states from those in which they were married This figure the editor interpreted as follows:

It does not mean, however, that any such proportion of these couples migrated for the purpose of being divorced; in fact, the migration of most of them doubtless may be accounted for by the general movement of population which takes place for economic and other reasons not connected with the question of divorce. In 1920, 22 per cent of the native-born people of the United States were living outside of the states in which they were born. High proportions of non-resident divorces in some of the Western states may appear to suggest some tendency to migrate for the purpose of securing a divorce. It must be remembered, there has long been a pronounced migratory movement of population to most of these Western states. . . . The proportion of migrants in the adult population has undoubtedly exceeded this figure (22 per cent), because children are not so likely to migrate.[7]

One pointed digression on this migratory divorce issue concerns divorces granted to couples married in Canada. The Canadian provinces have exceedingly strict divorce laws. Thirty-six per cent of American divorces granted to foreigners in 1922 went to Canadians. It must be remembered that many Canadians migrated here after marriage, and divorced years later without any idea of evasion of their

[7] *U. S. Marriage and Divorce Report*, 1922, p. 22.

MIGRATORY DIVORCE

sovereign laws. However, only eight per cent of the foreign population is Canadian. Logically, this group should acquire only 8 per cent of the divorces granted to foreigners. The presumption, therefore, is that about three-fourths of the 1,400 divorces granted to Canadians in 1922 were of the evasive migratory nature.

Every decennial census from 1870 to 1920 showed that the non-resident population or persons living in other states than those in which they were born has been slightly over 20 per cent. The 1920 figure was 22 per cent. The 1900 census gave an interesting fact, namely, that almost one-half of these migrants were living in adjoining states.

Divorces granted to non-resident couples amount to 26 per cent of the total, while 22 per cent of the entire population is classified as non-resident. This difference of 4 per cent is a rough approximation to the amount of evasive divorce. However, one crude figure cannot be accurately subtracted from the other; since the former concerns married couples between wedlock and divorce, while the latter refers to individuals between birth and census enumeration. A more interesting indication is the fact that in 28 per cent of all divorces the husband was granted a non-resident divorce, while in 25 per cent of the cases it was given to the wife. Thus for non-resident divorces the separate domiciles of wives and husbands happened to be only 3 per cent, and perhaps gives a reasonably close estimate of the amount of migratory divorce in the total number. In order to refine this estimate for greater accuracy the records of several of the most liberal and the most conservative divorce states will be examined to ascertain whether there is any considerable migration from the latter to the former. With the exception of Nevada, what percentage of divorces is granted to people migrating from conservative states for the express purpose of evasive divorce? Persons living in states with strict

68   STATISTICAL ANALYSIS OF AMERICAN DIVORCE

divorce laws, who wish to evade these, can go to Nevada, Paris, Mexico or to neighboring states. The last resource is obviously most inviting to all who are not wealthy, namely, to be divorced across the borderline in an adjacent state.

A popular belief is that New Yorkers frequently indulge in migratory divorce because the New York State law is very stringent. The 1922 report shows that 6,400 divorces were granted to people married in New York State; 3,300 of these divorces were decreed in New York. That leaves 3,100 non-resident divorces; however, many people have left New York State and moved to other regions of the country, being divorced there years later.[8] Their purpose in moving to the other state was in no way related to divorce. These 3,100 cases constituted 48 per cent of all divorces granted in the United States in 1922 to couples who had once married in New York. However, 18 per cent of the people born in New York reside in other states; so apparently not more than 30 per cent of New York divorces could be of the migratory nature. It must be recalled that almost half of non-resident Americans are living in states contiguous to their native commonwealth. Consequently, one half the non-resident population figure, or about 9 per cent of non-resident divorces from New York should normally be found in adjoining states, such as Vermont, Massachusetts, Connecticut, New Jersey and Pennsylvania, if no evasive migration existed. However, 1,400 New York divorces or 22 per cent of the total occurred in these contiguous states; this is a surplus of 900 divorces, above the expected number, implying the migratory tendency. Half of New York's non-resident divorces in these adjacent states occurred in Pennsylvania, which has fairly liberal divorce laws and only one year residence requirement. The other four neighboring states have

[8] Figures on interstate migration, unrelated to divorce, are from U. S. Census, 1920, vol. ii, p. 622.

MIGRATORY DIVORCE

two or three years' residence requirement. Furthermore, a considerably higher divorce rate compared with the rest of the state of Pennsylvania is found in the northern counties bordering New York. It is, therefore, safe to conclude that these 900 divorces in states contiguous to New York or 17 per cent of the total divorces granted in America to persons once married in New York are of the migratory nature, after allowance has been made for 500 non-resident New York divorces in these same states due to a shifting population. Two hundred divorces in Nevada were granted to New Yorkers. Very few of them could be traced to a shifting of population, so these must be considered as migratory for the purpose of evading the New York State law. This number constitutes 3 per cent of divorces to New Yorkers. All together, then, for 1922, the last annual report on non-resident divorces, there were about 1,100 New York divorces in other states for purely evasive purposes, 200 in Nevada and 900 in states contiguous to New York. If a few hundred divorces are added for Paris and Mexico, all these may constitute 20 per cent migratory divorce for the Empire State. Since New York grants divorce only on adultery, it would probably be among the worst offenders in migratory divorce, if this practice existed to any extent

Recapitulating, the figures showed 52 per cent of New York divorces took place in New York, when the marriage likewise had been in New York. There was deducted 18 per cent as New York's normal emigrating population from the remaining 48 per cent. However, the editor of the government divorce report has pointed out that the migration of adults is more frequent than that of children, and it is logical that young married people are especially prone to migrate from state to state thus later enhancing the number of non-resident divorces. Migratory divorces in adjoining states plus those in Nevada, show that about one-fifth of

70 STATISTICAL ANALYSIS OF AMERICAN DIVORCE

New York divorce applicants evade their own strict law. The New York divorce rate is about one-fourth of the country's average If all the migratory divorces are added, the percentage would still be only one-third of the national average. This indicates that public opinion supports and obeys New York's strict divorce law fairly well; since the United States in 1922 had 149,000 divorces, and only 1,100 of them were contributed by fleeting migrants from New York.

The State of South Carolina prohibits divorce entirely. Do South Carolinians cross state border lines in order to secure evasive divorces? The number of South Carolinians divorced in America represents .30 per thousand married population of South Carolina. This is only one-sixth of the divorce rate of the other South Atlantic states and about one-twelfth of the average American divorce rate. The fact is that 221 South Carolinians were divorced in other states during the year 1922. This number of non-resident divorces merely signifies the number of divorced couples once married in South Carolina. Now South Carolina happens to have a normal emigrating population of 16 per cent. If the people of South Carolina had the same proclivities toward divorce as inhabitants of the other South Atlantic states, then they would contribute about 16 per cent of non-resident divorces, assuming their state had the same divorce rate as its neighbors.

Of the 221 divorces, 87 took place in the bordering states of North Carolina and Georgia. North Carolina divorce laws are extremely strict, requiring three years' residence. This state had 53; Georgia, with lenient laws and only one year's residence, had 34; moreover, the northern counties of Georgia bordering South Carolina showed virtually no divorces at all. Only one South Carolina marriage ended in divorce in Nevada. The fact that more South Carolina marriages are divorced in North Carolina than in Georgia

MIGRATORY DIVORCE

merely shows a normal flow of population without any pronounced intention of divorce. These adjoining states had only 40 per cent of the South Carolina marriages which ended in divorce. Almost 50 per cent of state emigrants move to bordering states. If the divorce rate was high for migratory reasons, these two states would show much higher than 50 per cent of the non-resident divorces from South Carolina. As previously pointed out, the emigrant proportion of the general population from South Carolina is 16 per cent. Its 221 divorces, however, constitute a non-resident divorce rate of only 8 per cent, assuming hypothetically that South Carolina had the same divorce rate as the other South Atlantic states. This means that people married in South Carolina, who have moved to other states, account for a divorce rate only one-half of the normal non-resident divorce rate of the other states in America, where generally liberal divorce laws exist. The permanence of the marriage bond among South Carolina people is further emphasized by the fact that this state has one of the very lowest annulment rates in the nation.

From the extremely low figures for North Carolina, Georgia and Nevada, it is obvious that people married in South Carolina, who later move away, divorce only half as frequently in other states as their numbers allow. South Carolinians just do not divorce, at home or abroad. This astonishing fact may be doubted because some divorced persons, although very few, are living in South Carolina. Most of this class are Negroes, who migrate considerably as laborers in the Southern states. Moreover, it is obvious that people born, married and divorced in other states of this country sometimes move to South Carolina. Migratory divorce as a problem is infinitesimal for South Carolinians, and there is no proof in figures showing evasion of the state prohibition.

The District of Columbia grants divorce only upon the

72   STATISTICAL ANALYSIS OF AMERICAN DIVORCE

ground of adultery.   Four hundred and eighty-one divorces were granted in 1922 to people who were once married in the District of Columbia.   Only 84 were given in the District of Columbia itself.   One hundred and eighty were granted in the neighboring state of Virginia, where only one year's residence is required   Sixty-nine were decreed in Maryland where two years' residence is required.   All together 83 per cent of divorces granted to people married in the District of Columbia were non-resident divorces.   The emigrant population of Washington is about 29 per cent.   The figures must be scrutinized more closely.   Since about one-half of the non-resident population of Washington is located in the adjoining states of Virginia and Maryland, these states should have about 14 per cent of its emigrant population, and thus account for about 67 divorces normally.   However, they granted 249 divorces to people who had been married in the District of Columbia.   The presumption is that the surplus of 182 divorces is of the migratory character.   There can be added 8 more divorces of the District of Columbia marriages, which took place in Nevada, or a total of 190 evasive divorces.   This is about 40 per cent of the total divorces granted to people married in the District of Columbia, constituting its refined migratory divorce estimate.

The same procedure has been applied to New York and to South Carolina by analyzing neighboring state non-resident divorces and then adding Nevada divorces.   The migratory approximation for New York was about 20 per cent of the total divorces to New Yorkers: and for South Carolina, negligible.   The District of Columbia showed a fairly high estimate of 40 per cent, but the low absolute number does not make it of national consequence.   The reason for high migratory divorce from the District of Columbia as opposed to South Carolina and New York is obvious. The laws of South Carolina and New York are made by

MIGRATORY DIVORCE

legislatures, representing the public opinions of their constituents. If any substantial percentage of people evaded these strict laws, the legislatures would modify them in order to secure the divorce revenues for their own states On the other hand, the inhabitants of the District of Columbia submit to a congressional divorce law disregarding their own wishes as evidenced by migratory divorce.

North Carolina grants divorce upon adultery or five years' desertion. Consequently, the divorce rate is low, being only one-third of the American average. In 1922, 1,300 divorces were granted to people who had been married in North Carolina; 900 of these were decreed in that state. The remaining 400 were non-resident, but not necessarily migratory. Sixteen per cent of all people born in North Carolina were living in other states in 1920. This would account for one-half of these 400 cases. The other two hundred were probably migratory. Only ten North Carolinians were divorced in Tennessee, while 200 were divorced in Virginia. These states should be expected to attract the North Carolina population in about equal numbers. However, Tennessee has a two year residence requirement for divorce, while the Virginia residence is only one year. Hence one may assume that almost all of these latter divorces were of the evasive type, and also 18 Nevada divorces. Fifteen per cent of the divorces granted to people married in North Carolina, about 200 in number, were thus of the evasive, migratory nature. Even so, the North Carolina divorce rate would still be much below one-half the country's average. However, it must be remembered that in a state with strict laws, the migratory evil should express itself most strongly, so a 15 per cent migratory divorce figure for North Carolina is not serious from a national standpoint.

Louisiana, permitting divorce on adultery or seven years' separation, has one-half the national divorce rate. Of the

74   STATISTICAL ANALYSIS OF AMERICAN DIVORCE

two thousand divorces granted to persons once married in Louisiana, 1,600 were decreed in that state; 20 per cent were non-resident. Moreover, the number of emigrants from the state of Louisiana, now living in other parts of the country, also amounts to 20 per cent, according to the last decennial census. Inspection of the adjoining states of Arkansas, Texas and Mississippi shows extremely low divorce rates there to people married in other states; while Nevada records virtually no divorces from Louisiana. Consequently, there is no record, either in adjoining states or elsewhere, of evasive, migratory divorces for the people of old, conservative Louisiana

The great majority of state divorce codes, with few exceptions, are so liberal that it is needless to migrate across state boundary lines at considerable expense in time and money to seek a divorce.

After examination of the most conservative states, it is necessary to scrutinize the most liberal divorce states in the 1922 report. Oregon has a lenient divorce code, and ranks second in America in divorce frequency. Its rate is over twice the national average. Twenty-four hundred divorces were granted in Oregon in the year 1922; 1,100 were given to people married in Oregon; the remaining majority was thus non-resident. This does not mean that they came to Oregon for the purpose of migratory evasion. Practically no divorces in Oregon were from the half-dozen very strict jurisdictions in America. Washington with a still more liberal code of laws contributed 600 Oregon divorces. California gave 100 and Idaho 75. These aforementioned states are adjoining states, and large numbers of people married in Washington, California and Idaho just naturally move to Oregon, hardly for the purpose of divorce; since their own state laws are equally liberal. Slightly over half the population of Oregon was born in other states of

MIGRATORY DIVORCE

America, and that accounts for its high non-resident divorce rate. There is no evidence of evasive migration. Furthermore, 300 divorces were granted in other states, mostly Far Western, to people who were once married in Oregon. Again this merely shows that American population, especially in the Far West, is of a very shifting nature; and that few divorces are of the evasive, migratory character, compared to the large percentage of actual non-resident divorces.

Wyoming is another very lenient divorce state. A great many people are constantly moving to and from Wyoming, as its population is quite transient. This state granted about 500 divorces for 1922, and 200 of them were to people married in Wyoming. Over 100 were from the neighboring states of Colorado and Nebraska, both of which have very liberal divorce laws. Sixteen states contributed no divorce applicants to Wyoming, showing that it is not a migratory center. Since virtually all its divorces were granted to citizens of equally lenient commonwealths, it is reasonable to assume that the large number of non-resident divorces in Wyoming cannot be considered in any sense migratory. Moreover, about 40 per cent of the people married in Wyoming, who acquire divorces, are divorced outside their own liberal state, thus again illustrating the normal shifts of American population, especially westward.

Nevada is obviously a migratory divorce market. However, 1922 figures are not very helpful, because in 1927 Nevada decreased its residence period from six to three months, and thereby doubled its divorce frequency. In 1922, the 1019 divorces granted in Nevada, as distributed by place of marriage of the divorce plaintiff, showed New York first, California second, Nevada third, New Jersey fourth and Canada fifth. Evidently only a small percentage of Nevada divorces were bona-fide decrees to inhabitants of Nevada, even in 1922. One hundred and thirty-six were

76 STATISTICAL ANALYSIS OF AMERICAN DIVORCE

married in Nevada. However, Nevada had a non-resident population of 59 per cent. If this percentage is applied, there are an additional 203 divorced couples as bona-fide non-residents, totalling 339 valid resident Nevada divorces, or about one third the full number granted for 1922. This would be a local Nevada divorce percentage not much higher than Oregon or Wyoming, neither of which recruits divorce applicants.

The remaining divorces in Nevada, however, constituted about 68 per cent, meaning that two thirds were granted in the migratory fashion to people from other jurisdictions, who were evading their own state laws. Now by 1927 the Nevada divorce rate doubled, owing to the reduction of the residence clause to three months. Since the additional 1,500 divorce applicants in 1929 were probably all from other states, Nevada accounted for only one-sixth of its own divorces, while five-sixths were of the migratory character. Again one must point out that this is not an alarming problem since Nevada grants only 2,500 divorces annually. If five-sixths of these are migratory, this still shows that only 1 per cent of American divorces are attributed to Nevada's migratory output. Sensational newspaper accounts of wealthy persons have created erroneous impressions

Therefore, Nevada remains the outstanding exception in this migratory divorce bogey. With a population of less than 100,000, this state by enactment of lax laws, has become very pestiferous to other commonwealths in granting corporation charters, divorce decrees and marriage licenses with great liberality to anyone who will pay the price. When Nevada reduced its divorce residence requirement from six months to three months in 1927, it was calculated that it must double its rate of divorce to become a commercial success; the rate quickly doubled. Will Rogers calls Nevada " freedom's last stand." Reno has recently endeavored to

MIGRATORY DIVORCE

make divorce even more attractive by ordering secret decrees which are filed by number instead of name.

Within recent months the severe business depression of 1931 has goaded certain state legislatures to relax divorce residence requirements in order to gain revenues from the migratory divorce business. Laws were recently approved in Arkansas and Idaho to reduce the domicile period from one year to three months. Meanwhile Nevada has reduced its residence requirement to six weeks, which action was followed by a substantial increase in divorce.

For all other states one years' residence at least, and often several years, is required. Common sense tells one that very few people have sufficient money to live so long a period outside their own states for the purpose of evading divorce laws This fact is further accentuated by the high non-resident divorce rates of certain states where migration for evasive purposes would be useless. Thirteen per cent of New York divorces and 47 per cent of the District of Columbia divorces are granted to non-residents. One hundred and nineteen Minnesotans were divorced in Wisconsin; 117 Wisconsinians were divorced in Minnesota. Even 42 per cent of those divorce applicants once married in Nevada were divorced in other states. Pennsylvanians were divorced in forty-six states and people of forty-one states were divorced in Pennsylvania. Washington has an extremely liberal state divorce code, yet ten times as many Washingtonians were divorced in Oregon as were Oregonians in Washington. Such examples tend to show that the vast majority of non-resident divorces for couples married in one state and divorced in another are by no means migratory divorces for evasive purposes.

Finally what proportion of American divorces is obtained after migration for the purpose of evading state laws? Divorce is so simple in all but five states that a considerable

78   STATISTICAL ANALYSIS OF AMERICAN DIVORCE

amount of migration would be futile.   Granted that Nevada attracts over 2,000 divorcees, that Paris and Mexico combined obtain a few hundred, that more than 1,000 New Yorkers cross to immediately adjoining states for divorce, and that a few hundred inhabitants of the District of Columbia and North Carolina do likewise, this total would be only about 4,000 or 2 per cent of American divorces.   For generous measure one may add a liberal estimate of an additional 1 per cent for the remaining forty-five states   A three per cent migratory estimate for divorce would be just the 3 per cent difference between the husband and wife percentages for non-resident divorces given in the 1922 divorce report, which was assumed to be a fair approximation.   The incontrovertible evidence is strikingly clear, that of about 200,000 American divorces annually, only a small fraction belongs to the evasive, migratory class.

CHAPTER VI

LAWS AND THE HOME

A widespread belief is that both marriage and divorce laws strongly influence the number of divorces in this country. There are forty-eight different marriage and divorce codes for the states plus the federal code for the District of Columbia. This chapter will analyze first the effect of state marriage laws upon divorce, second the influence of state divorce laws, and third the proposal for a uniform federal divorce code.

The late Professor George E. Howard of the University of Nebraska, author of a monumental three-volume work, *A History of Matrimonial Institutions,* strongly believed American marriage laws to be at the root of the divorce evil. First Dr Howard stated what he termed the imaginary causes of divorce.[1]

(1) Imperfect administration and faulty judicial procedure are not the principal causes of divorce.

(2) Interstate migration for divorce has not noticeably raised the divorce rate.

(3) Liberal divorce laws do not perceptibly raise the rate, and do not invite divorce.

(4) Divorced persons do not remarry much faster than widows or widowers.

(5) America's divorce record does not indicate a low domestic morality.

[1] Howard, *The Family and Marriage* (Lincoln, Neb., 1914). sections xxiii-xxiv.

79

80   STATISTICAL ANALYSIS OF AMERICAN DIVORCE

Professor Howard believed that bad marriage laws and bad marriages are the most dangerous of the various social conditions causing divorce   He wrote as follows:

What proper check does society place upon the marriage of the unfit?   Is there any boy or girl so immature if only the legal age of consent has been reached; is there any delinquent so dangerous through inherited tendencies, disease or crime; is there any worn-out debauchee, who cannot somewhere find a magistrate to tie the sacred knot? [2]

Dr. Howard further stated, " The defects in the matrimonial laws of the United States are many and grave; but perhaps the chief obstacle in the way of securing a proper social control is the general recognition of the validity of the so-called common-law marriage." [3]

Gretna Green is any marriage market, possessing a parson or justice of the peace with a genial leniency toward matrimony, in a state with lax marriage laws across the border-line from a state where strictness prevails [4]   Professor Howard believed that Gretna Greens are more fruitful of divorces than divorce colonies.   He finally added, " Divorce is the medicine for the disease of marriage, but the principal fountain of divorce is bad matrimonial laws and bad marriage." [5]   Dr. Howard urged positive steps to cure the marriage evils.[6]

(1) Abolish common law marriages.
(2) Unify consanguineity laws.

[2] Howard, *A History of Matrimonial Institutions* (Chicago, 1904), vol. iii, p 254.

[3] *Ibid.*, vol. iii, p. 170.

[4] The original Gretna Green was a Scotch village just across the English border, a haven for eloping couples

[5] *Ibid.*

[6] *The Family and Marriage*, sections xxiii-xxiv.

LAWS AND THE HOME
81

(3) Raise age of marriage to eighteen for girls and twenty-one for men.

(4) Make obligatory civil service, modern license and registration system, and publication of civil banns.

(5) Bar marriage of the unfit

This analysis of defects in American marriage laws has been stated in detail because of the prevalent belief concerning their importance in accounting for America's high divorce rate. Nevertheless, the tendency of marriage legislation from the Civil War to the present time has been one of greater stringency, while the divorce rate has advanced uniformly just the same.

Mary E. Richmond and Fred S. Hall recently published an analysis of American state marriage laws for the Russell Sage Foundation.[7] A major fact is that all states now require a minimum age limit of eighteen for both bride and groom unless the parental consent of both applicants has been given. It is popularly believed that young marriages are most fruitful in providing divorces, but for many decades the legal age of marriage has steadily risen.

The latest available decennial census gives the percentage of divorced persons in the total population.[8] Although this number is admittedly under-estimated, there is no reason to believe that the percentages of divorced persons in the total population by various age groupings are peculiarly biased in numbers for any particular age group. In other words, it may be assumed that the under-estimate is similar for all age subdivisions of the population. To the total married population of the United States over fifteen years of age, the number of divorced persons bears a ratio of 1.18 per

[7] Richmond and Hall, *Marriage and the State* (New York, 1929), p. 370.

[8] *U. S. Census*, 1920, vol. ii, p. 388.

82 STATISTICAL ANALYSIS OF AMERICAN DIVORCE

cent. There happen to be comparatively few persons either married or divorced under the age of fifteen, but if these very young marriages tend especially toward divorce, the ratio of divorced to married persons under fifteen years would obviously be higher than 1.18 per cent for the population over fifteen years in this classification by age groups. This ratio is just 1.05 per cent for the group under fifteen years of age The ratio of divorced to married persons from fifteen to nineteen years of age, inclusive, was .97 per cent For the age group twenty to twenty-four years, inclusive, the ratio is 1.04 per cent. These figures indicate that young marriages have a slightly lower divorce frequency than the total marriages of the general population

Many of the difficulties of marriage laws are practically beyond social control. It is incalculably easier to avoid the marriage laws of a state by crossing its boundary line into another state for a few minutes than to evade a divorce law by establishing a year or more of residence in an adjoining state. Concerning the restrictions of marriages of mentally unfit, Richmond and Hall write, " The difficulty of effecting any control of mental defect or transmissible disease by means of marriage laws is very great " [9]

Nevertheless, an attempt will be made to correlate divorce rates of states with their present marriage laws.[10] According to data given in Richmond and Hall, a number of states forbid evasion of their own marriage laws by refusing to recognize the legality of wedlock contracted outside the state, which would not have been valid under the state's own marriage laws.[11] Since these states are more stringent, they

[9] Richmond and Hall, *Marriage and the State*, p 59.

[10] Since the rates constitute a statistical variable, while the laws are in the category of an attribute, this requires a non-quantitative method of correlation known as bi-serial r. See Rietz, *Handbook of Mathematical Statistics*, pp 136-137.

[11] Richmond and Hall, *Marriage and the State*, p. 370.

LAWS AND THE HOME   83

ought then perhaps to show lower divorce rates. The correlation between these marriage laws and the state divorce rates for 1929 as expected is negative, but the coefficient is so low, —.19, that it would be impossible from the statistical evidence to attribute a marked effect on the divorce rate to this type of law.[12]

The majority of states require no advance notice for a marriage ceremony. If lax marriage laws of this type produce high divorce rates, the correlation between the marriage laws and divorce rates of those states for 1929 should be high and positive. The coefficient is of moderate size, + .45, indicating to a limited extent that hasty marriages have a tendency to end in divorce.

About half the states permit common-law marriages. The correlation between these state marriage laws and divorce rates for 1929 gives a coefficient ⊥ .18, the statistical evidence indicating no significant association between common-law marriage and the divorce rate.

There seems to be no substantial evidence that the American family ills can be cured by reforming the marriage laws. As previously stated, the tendency of marriage legislation has been one of increasing strictness for many decades. This denotes its ineffectiveness in combating the advancing divorce rate.

A survey of the influence of state divorce laws on the American divorce rate is now in order. The general policy of divorce legislation in the United States from the Civil War to the present time must be briefly reviewed. Dr. Caroll D. Wright analyzed the existing divorce legislation of 1867.[13] The various jurisdictions granted divorce on the following grounds: forty-seven states and territories

[12] These correlations are based on thirty-nine states, the standard divorce area explained in a former chapter.

[13] U. S. Marriage and Divorce Report, 1867-1886, ch i.

34   STATISTICAL ANALYSIS OF AMERICAN DIVORCE

allowed divorce for adultery, forty-five on desertion, forty-one for cruelty, thirty-nine on imprisonment, thirty-seven for habitual drunkenness and twenty-seven on neglect to provide.

Contrast this with the present jurisdictions on divorce forty-eight allow divorce for adultery, forty-six on desertion, forty-four for cruelty, forty for drunkenness, forty for imprisonment and twenty-seven for neglect to provide. It appears that major legal changes have been surprisingly few during the six decades of a fivefold advance of the divorce rate.

However, there has been considerable divorce legislative activity for the entire sixty-three years. Every year several states modify their divorce laws and experiment with different provisions, although comparatively few changes have been of a serious nature. The general tendency of divorce laws has been toward increasing strictness. At one time during the early period eight states permitted divorce by the famous omnibus clause, which means any ground upon the discretion of the judge. To-day no state allows the omnibus. At one time nine states and territories permitted divorce upon less than a year's residence and thus encouraged people to migrate to those states for divorces. Nevada is the only jurisdiction to-day which will grant divorce to parties who have resided in the state for less than a year. Other legal changes in divorce have been few, but likewise have tended toward increasing stringency. South Carolina had a divorce law just after the Civil War, but it was soon repealed. The District of Columbia permitted divorce on several grounds before the year 1899, but Congress revised its divorce code, allowing only infidelity as a ground under the new law.

At present only six of the forty-nine jurisdictions have legal divorce regulations significantly distinct from the re-

LAWS AND THE HOME

85

maining states. Nevada is notoriously lax on account of its six weeks' residence requirement despite the fact that the legal grounds for divorce in Nevada are about the same as those of other states. South Carolina permits no divorce; New York and the District of Columbia grant divorce solely on the ground of infidelity; North Carolina and Louisiana are likewise strict, permitting divorce only for infidelity and for desertion of five years in the former state and seven years in the latter state. Divorce laws of the remaining forty-three states in this country are fairly uniform and lenient. Professor Willcox wrote recently," Those causes enacted into laws by various state legislatures indicate the pleas which have been endorsed by the social judgments of the respective communities." [14]

An endeavor will be made to discover by the review of previous writings and the analysis of recent legislation whether changes in the divorce laws of states have constituted a substantial cause of increasing American divorce.

In his doctoral dissertation at Columbia University in 1891, Walter F. Willcox analyzed in detail the effects of legal changes upon various state divorce rates during the period from 1867 to 1886. His conclusions were: "In five states the number of divorces was unaffected by legislation which had occurred; five states showed slight temporary changes; two states only were permanently influenced by divorce legislation, and in these states the number of divorces had not been numerically large." [15] His summary follows:

Yet after giving due weight to these exceptions, it must be admitted that the influence of law, if not nil, is at least much less than commonly supposed. The proposed modes of reduc-

[14] Willcox, "Divorce in the U. S.," *Encyclopedia Britannica*, vol. viii, p. 460.

[15] Willcox, *The Divorce Problem, a Study in Statistics*, p 55.

STATISTICAL ANALYSIS OF AMERICAN DIVORCE

ing divorce by law may be classified as retrictions on marriage, restrictions on divorce and restrictions on remarriage. Restrictions on marriage reduce the number of marriages and thus ultimately the number of divorces. The attendant evils are so great, nevertheless, as to make such restrictions unwise. Restrictions on remarriage would probably not reduce the number of divorces. The statistical evidence obtainable indicates that divorces are not sought in order to remarry. Restrictions on divorce exert a minor influence on the divorce rate. The only effective method of reducing the number of divorces would be to raise the cost of divorce and thus discriminate between rich and poor applicants. The conclusion of the whole matter is that law can do little. The immediate, direct, and measurable influence of legislation is subsidiary, unimportant, almost imperceptible [16]

Dr. Willcox's analysis of the effects of legislation for the first twenty-year period of divorce records has been substantiated by later findings. The doctoral dissertation of James P. Lichtenberger at Columbia University in 1909 investigated the legal changes for both marriage and divorce and their effects upon the divorce rates of various states for the second twenty-year period of American divorce statistics, specifically for the years 1887-1906. Professor Lichtenberger wrote as follows:

Assuming with many students of social science that the phenomenon is rather but one aspect of a general social movement whose roots lie deep in the soil of physical processes and is not amenable, therefore, to the external forces of social control. . . .

Purposive efforts to check the movement have centered in more rigid enforcement of ecclesiastical discipline and more stringent enactments and administration of civil law. Despite these efforts, the divorce rate has continued to advance with accelerated velocity [17]

[16] Willcox, *The Divorce Problem, a Study in Statistics*, p. 61.

[17] Lichtenberger, *Divorce a Study in Social Causation*, p. 5.

LAWS AND THE HOME 87

During that twenty-year period, one hundred and eight marriage and divorce laws were passed, only seven being relaxations. Following the publication of the first *U. S. Marriage and Divorce Report* in 1889, state legislatures began to bustle with activity to reform the marriage and divorce situation. Nevertheless, a continued advance in the divorce rate and also a rise in the marriage rate persisted.

Professor Lichtenberger gave the following summary concerning the effects of several state laws restricting remarriage of divorced persons:

The result of legal changes restricting remarriage was not sufficient to retard the general marriage rate in eleven of the fifteen states which passed such legislation: for these states showed a positive increase in the number of marriages in the year following such enactments. The decrease in two of the others occurred in 1894, when the marriage rate for the entire country was diminished on account of the financial depression. In one other case, that of Kansas, the restriction was so slight as to be practically of no consequence, leaving only one state, California, for which no other explanation is apparent. The general marriage rate only slightly declined for the year following the enactment and regained the normal rate in the second year.[18]

Five states enacted laws for the defense of the absent party at a divorce trial, but the percentage of denials in four of these fell below the average percentage for the United States; so this legislation was not a determining factor in decreasing divorce.

Of eighteen states that increased the divorce residence requirement, only two showed substantial, permanent decreases in the divorce rate. On the other hand, five states relaxed their residence requirement without changing the general trends of their divorce rates.

[18] Lichtenberger, *Divorce a Study in Social Causation*, p. 108.

88 STATISTICAL ANALYSIS OF AMERICAN DIVORCE

Finally, Dr. Lichtenberger analyzed the various effects of changes in the legal grounds for divorce, and found that only six states showed positive effects of divorce law modification, and here numerical results were negligible and temporary. For the entire period the only substantial changes in divorce rates, which were directly attributable to laws, occurred in South Dakota where a three months' residence requirement was changed to a year, consequently causing decreasing divorce; and in the District of Columbia, where three divorce grounds were repealed and one substituted in its place, again lowering the divorce rate. Both of these jurisdictions, due to their small populations, contributed a very minor percentage to the national divorce total. Dr. Lichtenberger's conclusions were that changes in legal regulations of marriage, divorce or remarriage were ineffective in influencing the divorce rate.[19]

Since annual divorce surveys were not taken during the next fifteen years, the effect of legislative activity cannot be traced till the period from 1922 to 1928, inclusive. Here a final attempt is undertaken to discover whether state legal changes contributed to increasing divorce during the most recent years.

The latest information on legal changes is compiled by the United States Legislative Reference Bureau at the Congressional Library. Their index of state laws shows that about one-half the states have altered their divorce laws within the seven-year period, 1922-1928. Most of these changes, however, have been of a technical nature concerning jurisdiction and minor modifications about alimony and property rights of women. A number of states have had substantial changes in their divorce laws, nevertheless, which might potentially affect their divorce rates. These will be examined in alphabetical order.

[19] Lichtenberger, *Divorce a Study in Social Causation*, pp. 109-113.

LAWS AND THE HOME 89

In 1925 a Colorado law decreed that remarriage could not take place until six months after the divorce trial. The several years following this enactment merely showed a normal increase in the divorce rate.

In 1927 Delaware enacted that all divorce trials should be secret, and also allowed divorce on the ground of non-support. During the next two years no inhabitant of Delaware took advantage of this latter ground. Instead of an increase in divorces due to the privacy in hearings, Delaware's divorce rate has declined.

Illinois in 1923 repealed the law that prohibited remarriage within a year of divorce. There was a temporary increase of divorces following this enactment, but the rate soon became stabilized.

Louisiana in 1925 allowed divorce on the additional ground of disease, and Minnesota in 1927 permitted divorce for insanity. The number of divorces since granted upon these two grounds in Louisiana and Minnesota has been negligible.

In 1925 a Nebraska law decreed that six months' notice of service of suit must precede a divorce trial. The years previous to 1925 had shown a declining divorce rate in Nebraska. This new law was of course intended to decrease divorce. Paradoxically, a sustained increase then commenced.

New Jersey in 1923 allowed divorce on the ground of extreme cruelty. Since that date, less than one-tenth of the total divorces in New Jersey has ever been granted during any year on the ground of cruelty, and the general trend of the state's total divorce rate was unchanged. In 1927 New Jersey enacted a law that the preliminary divorce decree did not become absolute for three months; nevertheless, the increase of divorces remained at a normal rate for the following years. The legislature of New Jersey has thus

90 STATISTICAL ANALYSIS OF AMERICAN DIVORCE

enacted two legal changes, one strengthening and one loosen-
ing the rigidity of the divorce statute, but neither had
practical effects

In 1922 New York enacted a law permitting divorce on
the ground of desertion; provided that one's spouse had
been missing for five years, and that all evidence pointed to
the disappearance or death of same.   Less than one-tenth of
New York divorces during any one year has since been
granted upon that ground, and the total divorce rate for the
state has merely shown a normal increase.

Nevada in 1927 reduced its residence requirement from
six months to three.   The divorce rate doubled and has
since remained at the new high level.

North Dakota in 1927 changed its law so as to permit a
partial divorce in place of its former separate maintenance
suit.   The following years showed just the normal increase
in the state divorce rate.

Oklahoma in 1927 decreed that remarriage could not take
place until six months after the divorce.   Instead of the
expected decline in the divorce rate, a divorce increase
occurred there during the ensuing years.

The Oregon legislature during the year 1927 passed a law
requiring the district attorney of each county to be the
defendant for the state in every divorce case which was uncontested.   In this state a steady decline in the divorce rate
occurred.

During 1925 South Dakota permitted divorce for incur-
able insanity, but a negligible number of divorce cases has
since occurred upon that ground.

Vermont in 1927 enacted that a decree *nisi* does not become absolute until six months have expired.   The object
here again was to prevent immediate remarriage.   The
divorce rate of Vermont remained nearly stationary during
the next few years in about the same manner as previously.

LAWS AND THE HOME

The summary of recent divorce legislation shows that fourteen states enacted sixteen legal changes of note during the seven years from 1922-1928 inclusive. Ten alterations may be called relaxations and six can be classified as restrictions. The effect of these legal changes on the divorce rate was:

Five instances showed no change.

Five showed negligible influences of law.

In one state, a temporary increase resulted from a legal liberalization.

In three states, the reverse trend of the divorce rate occurred from that expected as a result of the legal change.

Two states only showed positive changes of the divorce rate in concurrence with the modifications of the laws.

The net result of legislation on divorce rates during the recent 1922 to 1928 period is negligible.

In order to test the variability of the divorce rates of states where laws are reasonably similar, a sample was selected of the twelve central states for 1928: Illinois, Indiana, Iowa, Kansas, Michigan, Minnesota, Missouri, Nebraska, North Dakota, Ohio, South Dakota and Wisconsin. These states are fairly homogeneous in both legal and religious aspects, as well as in their ethnic composition. A ratio of dispersion showed a high degree of variability and probably indicated instability of underlying causes from state to state during the year 1928.[20] The variation in laws could not explain a fraction of this decided heterogeneity in divorce rates.

A composite divorce rate of the Pacific, Rocky Mountain and Southwestern states is three times the composite divorce rate of the New England, Middle Atlantic and South At-

[20] The Lexis ratio showed the distribution to be supernormal giving a high coefficient 83.9. See Rietz, *Handbook of Mathematical Statistics*, pp. 89-91.

STATISTICAL ANALYSIS OF AMERICAN DIVORCE

lantic states. The central states, both north and south, have a medium divorce rate between these two extremes. Since all but six states have substantially uniform divorce codes, widely divergent divorce rates of states must be explained by other factors.

This is simple to exemplify. Georgia has ten grounds for divorce, while Florida with nine, has five times the divorce rate. Kansas and Oklahoma have identical divorce codes, but the Oklahoma rate is 50 per cent higher. Vermont with five grounds for divorce has a higher rate than Rhode Island with eleven. All these foregoing figures make manifest that divorce laws rarely influence the percentages of divorces granted.

A detailed analysis and summary of divorce legislation from the Civil War to the present time shows that the number of changes has been many, but their importance slight, because the divorce laws to-day are not substantially different from those of sixty-three years ago. However, there has been a minor tendency toward increasing strictness. Since the divorce rate has multiplied fivefold notwithstanding, the legal influences evidently were negligible. Examples shown in the previous pages, where states have endeavored to change the course of their divorce rates by legislative reforms, point with few exceptions to futility in influencing the number of divorces. Therefore, the conclusion is inevitable that legal changes do not constitute a substantial cause of increasing divorce.

Since state laws have failed to check the divorce rate, there has been a considerable agitation to enact a uniform federal divorce law. The Sanctity of Marriage Association has strongly urged a constitutional amendment on divorce.[21] It claims support of many organizations:

[21] *Sanctity of Marriage Association*, Bulletin No. viii, September, 1923.

LAWS AND THE HOME 93

American Bar Association
General Assembly of the Presbyterian Church
General Federation of Women's Clubs
International Reform Bureau
Methodist Episcopal Church
National Education Association
National Lutheran Council
National Reform Association
National Women's Temperance Union
Triennial Episcopal General Convention

President Roosevelt's recommendation in a message to Congress in 1906 is the keynote: " The census of divorce is fairly appalling. Easy divorce is a bane to any nation: it is a curse to society and a menace to the home, an incitement to married unhappiness; an evil thing for men and a still more hideous thing for women."

The editorial staff of the *Pictorial Review Magazine* has been a most enthusiastic sponsor of a federal divorce law; in fact, the reform element of the country has rallied to a large extent behind this proposed panacea for American divorce ills. One zealous writer on the subject is the Reverend Franklin E. Parker of Boston, who crusades as follows:

> Hark Ye! lawyers and judges
> But should you seek divorce and break
> Your oath and marriage tie forsake.
> How then can you expect support—
> From God divine of any sort?
> As when you seek to gain divorce.
> You reap the thistles of remorse.[22]

The International Reform Bureau has already boasted of the effectiveness of its lobbying activities before Congress

[22] Parker, *Marriage and Divorce with a Soul Understanding* (Boston, 1923), p. 30.

94   *STATISTICAL ANALYSIS OF AMERICAN DIVORCE*

in making more stringent the divorce law of the District of Columbia and the divorce statutes of the federal territories.[23] Since the District of Columbia grants divorce only upon the ground of infidelity, perhaps that is the reason why advocates of strict divorce are anxious for federal regulation.

The first uniform divorce bill was introduced into Congress in 1884, but none has ever emerged from committee docket. In 1892 the Report of the Judiciary Committee of the United States House of Representatives dismissed this proposed amendment with the statement that it was an " invasion of the domestic rights of the people " for Congress to enact uniform marriage and divorce laws.[24]

Upon the request of President Roosevelt a national congress on uniform divorce laws was held at Washington in 1906. Thirty-three states were represented and the unanimous decision of the convention was " that no federal divorce law is feasible, and that all efforts to secure the passage of such a constitutional amendment would be futile." [25] This congress on uniform divorce laws adopted a model code, which it urged the states to ratify, but only three states took legal action.

The champions of a uniform, federal divorce law to be sanctioned by constitutional amendment see two distinct benefits to be gained by this unique step in legislation affecting American home life. First, the supposed evil of interstate migratory divorce would be eliminated. Second, the more emphatic aim of the reform elements sponsoring a uniform divorce law is to combat the growing evil of American divorce and by the aid of the strong arm of Congressional legislation to preserve the family.

[23] See *Patriotic Studies*, Int. Reform Bureau, Washington, D. C, 1906.

[24] *House Resolution 46*, May 5, 1892, 52nd Cong., 1st Sess., House Report, 1290.

[25] *Proceedings of the National Congress on Uniform Divorce Laws* (Harrisburg, 1906), p. 57.

LAWS AND THE HOME

The latest uniform divorce law proposal, as advocated by Senator Capper, is a composite code of present state legislation. It names six grounds for divorce, which are now existent in almost all the states, including Nevada This plan would achieve the first aim of its proponents by eliminating the minor matter of interstate migratory divorce, which a detailed factual analysis in the previous chapter showed to amount to only 3 per cent of the grand total. Second, this composite divorce code would extend liberal divorce laws to the District of Columbia, Louisiana, New York, North Carolina and South Carolina, thus creating the opportunities in these conservative states for slight divorce increases. Thus the second and chief aim of the reform elements sponsoring uniform divorce laws, namely, to reduce the growing divorce evil, would in no way be accomplished by adopting the typical divorce legislation of the states as the provisions of a federal code. On the other hand, the imposition by Congress of a uniform divorce law upon a country where diverse conditions of family life exist may be fraught with attendant disadvantages.

At present, forty-eight different state viewpoints representing public opinions underlie the forty-eight different state laws. By the principle of home rule and local self-government, the states rather than Congress are in more intimate touch with the personal affairs of the American family. The South Carolina law represents the public opinion of that state. From 1872 to 1878 the "carpet bag" legislature allowed divorce in that state, but it was abolished as soon as the white lawmakers returned to power. Nevada reënacted by referendum in 1913 its liberal divorce residence requirement after the legislature had repealed it. South Dakota and Oregon legislatures attempted to make divorce stricter, but were overruled by referenda to the people. A federal divorce law would deprive the country of

96 STATISTICAL ANALYSIS OF AMERICAN DIVORCE

forty-eight experimental laboratories in social legislation, which provide the primary sources of improvement. Every year a few states modify their divorce laws, several dozen legal changes occurring every decade. Divorce in America is still a flexible and changing problem, unready for a standardized legal solution.

The proposed federal divorce amendment to the United States Constitution would permit a composite code of the strict and liberal states of this country. This is socially unsound, because it would mean an unsatisfactory compromise of principle, distasteful to all states who were compelled to abide by it against their wishes and a sacrifice of ideals by both liberal and stringent states. If the legal standards of progressive states are forcibly lowered and those of backward states likewise raised, the average code may result in a meaningless muddle. A federal law as a compromise would penalize progressive states. The future standard is often fixed by the state which pioneers and ventures on new experiments. A new law is tried by a particular state. If it fails in results, it is repealed; if successful, it is adopted by other states. This compromise code would deprive the nation of values existing under the present system by destroying the forty-eight experimental laboratories where social improvements are evolved. Diversity of conditions underlies the diversity of law. How can unity of laws reasonably be forced where no unity of opinions exist? Congress seems to realize this by the diversity of divorce laws in its own jurisdiction. Alaska grants divorce on six grounds; Hawaii, seven: Porto Rico, eight; and the District of Columbia, one. All of these are fixed by congressional legislation. The District of Columbia, granting divorce only on the ground of adultery, is an example of congressional legislation. On this basis, should one wish to intrust Congress with the moral affairs of the American

LAWS AND THE HOME

family? A federal law could be altered only with great inconvenience. Such changes could not be based on scientific experiment. A poor state law has little effect, but the whole nation might suffer from a federal legal blunder. Law is created from experience.

National uniformity of divorce laws is strenuously advocated by well-intentioned but uninformed people, who are grasping blindly for a remedy to preserve the American home. However, about forty-three states now have substantial uniformity of laws. A federal law would decrease the migratory divorce rate in very lenient Nevada, but might lead to divorce increases where the extremely strict divorce laws of the District of Columbia, Louisiana, New York, North Carolina and South Carolina would be substituted by a federal divorce code of a compromise nature. Therefore, any uniform divorce law representing public opinion as now asserted by the divorce laws of the great majority of states, could not decrease the total amount of divorce. A congressional law would be socially unsound as an unsatisfactory compromise, penalizing progressive states and establishing a stagnant legal situation with slight opportunity of improvement. It would destroy forty-eight experimental laboratories in the states that are adapting new laws to new circumstances in the divorce problem. No commission of experts knows the moral and expedient provisions for a federal code, and the American family is still unprepared for any such fixed and arbitrary standard.

This chapter has reviewed the failure of state marriage laws and state divorce laws to effect substantially the persistent fivefold increase in the American divorce rate during the past six decades and also the futility of the proposed panacea of uniform, federal divorce laws. Law contemplates specific remedies; but divorce is the result of a complex of causes, which legislation can do little to modify.

CHAPTER VII

REMARRIAGE

A third popular notion is that desire for remarriage is a fundamental factor in the divorce problem in addition to migratory divorce and marriage and divorce legislation. It is essential to investigate this phenomenon to disclose whether changes in the frequency of remarriage are a contributory cause of increasing divorce.

Do the great majority of divorce applicants rend the marriage bonds asunder for the prime purpose of remarrying, or are they already too badly discouraged by one domestic failure to attempt another? On the contrary, perhaps it is those that have tried it most frequently, who are convinced marriage is a failure. As previously discovered, state laws prohibiting or delaying remarriage have not succeeded in lowering divorce rates.

A number of years ago, Dr. Joseph A. Hill of the United States Census Bureau, analyzed the rates of remarriage for divorcees listed in the second government report, 1887-1906. The comparatively few figures showed about 28 per cent remarriage in Rhode Island, 37 per cent in Connecticut and 33 per cent in Maine. Dr. Hill commented as follows:

That a certain proportion of divorced persons should remarry is as natural and inevitable as for the widowed. Divorcees are usually younger than widowed persons.

That case in which A divorces B in order to marry C may not be unusual, but it is certainly not typical of the great majority of divorce cases; on the contrary, it probably represents only a small proportion of the total number of divorces granted.[1]

[1] Hill, " Statistics of Divorce," *Quarterly Publications of the American Statistical Association*, June, 1909, p. 494.

REMARRIAGE 99

On the basis of these statistics just quoted the Reverend Dr. Dike, eminent divorce reformer, likewise believed that the remarriage rates were hardly any higher for divorced persons than for widowed persons.

Professor Walter F. Willcox wrote recently on this subject:

A statement frequently made regarding divorce in the United States, which does not find warrant in the statistics on the subject, is that the real motive for divorce is the desire for remarriage to a third person.

In Connecticut, however, for a number of years information as to previous marriage was required; and if the statements were trustworthy, the number of persons remarrying each year was about one-third the total number of persons divorcing, which is probably a rate not widely different from widows and widowers of the same age. What statistical evidence there is on the subject therefore tends to discredit the popular opinion.[2]

Dr. Willard Waller of the University of Nebraska, after investigation of case studies of a considerable number of divorced persons, tacitly approved the census figure for 1906, which estimated that about one-third of the divorced persons remarried.[3]

The number of divorces granted every year is accurately stated; but the number of divorced persons living in the general population is most dubious, even though every decennial census since 1890 has enumerated divorced persons. Some popular writers on the subject of divorce have compared this number of divorced persons, which is fairly small, with the high number of divorces granted annually; and have decided that divorced persons either die or remarry

[2] Willcox, " Divorce in the U. S.," *Encyclopedia Britannica*, vol. viii, p. 460.

[3] Waller, *The Old Love and the New* (New York, 1930), statistical appendix.

rather rapidly, with the inference toward the latter. Neither implication is justified.

Every census editor has admitted that the number of divorced persons stated in the decennial census is woefully inadequate. Either an individual or the housekeeper gives the record of one's marital status to the census enumerator. It is natural that many divorced persons, for reasons of embarrassment, list themselves under the classification. single, married or widowed. This reasoning is corroborated by authority. The decennial census editor for 1920 wrote as follows: " Moreover, it is probable that some divorced persons are erroneously reported single, some as married and some as widowed, so that the census return understates somewhat the actual number of divorced persons who have not remarried." [4] This obvious condition is reflected in the following ditty:

> Still the census taker tarried
> With a poised and ready pen;
> ' One more question, Are you married?'
> Came the answer, ' Now and then.'

The 1920 decennial census listed 509.000 persons as divorced, or only about 36 divorced persons for every ten divorces granted that year.[5] In 1890 the relative ratio of divorced persons to divorces was 37 to 10, a negligible difference from 1920, considering the rapid increase of the divorce rate during that period. If there had been any great acceleration of remarriages among divorced persons over this thirty year period, obviously this relationship could not remain stationary.

The enumeration of 509,000 divorced persons was for January 1, 1920. Now for the year 1919, an estimated

[4] *U. S. Census*, 1920, vol. ii, p. 383.

[5] *U. S. Census*, 1920, vol. ii, p. 390.

REMARRIAGE

141,500 divorces were granted by the courts of this country, thus creating 283,000 divorced persons in one year alone. Simple arithmetic shows that such a yearly number of newly divorced persons must die or remarry within 1.8 years or exceed the decennial census count of divorced persons. Unless all of the divorcees for each given year could remarry or die within one year and ten months after their divorces were granted, they would more than equal the number of persons divorced as enumerated in the census of 1920. It is unbelievable that death and remarriage could be at such a rapid rate; therefore it is more plausible to agree with the census editor when he declares the number of divorced persons to be underestimated.

Professor Ogburn thinks that the percentage of divorced persons who do not remarry must be large. He arrived at such conclusion from an analysis of the New York State figures of 1916 when 3,500 divorces were granted.[6] The state records on this subject of remarriage showed that about 1,800 divorced persons remarried that year. However, considerable numbers of New York divorces, probably about 20 per cent, were granted in other states, consequently boosting the total of New York divorcees above 4,000. Moreover, the records showed that three and four-tenths years was the average time elapsing between divorce and the remarriage of divorced persons. The New York rate thus showed that about 40 per cent of divorced persons remarried, but this was accentuated out of proportion by the high remarriage rate of divorced persons in New York City. If the New York rate was applied to the rest of the nation, it would show that the length of time between divorce and death or remarriage would be only one and eight-tenth years in the United States, provided the decennial census figure for population of di-

[6] Groves and Ogburn, *American Marriage and Family Relationships*, pp. 363-365.

102 *STATISTICAL ANALYSIS OF AMERICAN DIVORCE*

vorcees was accurate. However, the New York records showed that three and four-tenth years elapsed between divorce and the average remarriage, so the federal figures for the national divorced population present a misleading underestimate. Even though one assumes that 40 per cent of New York divorcees remarry, the conservative divorce state of New York where marital dissolutions are granted only upon infidelity, does not by any means represent the national problem for remarriage of divorced persons.

The weight of evidence, although actual facts are lacking to a large extent on the problem of remarriage, seems to indicate from the viewpoints of such authorities as Hill, Dike, Willcox, Waller and Ogburn, that the popular notion of frequent remarriage of divorced persons is very much exaggerated.

Contrary to these facts and opinions, Dr. I. M. Rubinow, a former government and social insurance statistician, has arrived at the sensational conclusion that the desire for remarriage is probably the primary cause for divorce. Just a few years ago he estimated that about 80 per cent of divorced persons remarry excluding those who die soon after divorce.[7] His monistic interpretation was quoted at length in the *International Yearbook* for 1928.

Dr. Rubinow extended this idea still more recently in an article entitled, " After Divorce, What? " as follows:

A careful computation taking into account the number of divorced persons at the beginning and the number in the end of each year, the number of divorced persons dying during the year, and the number of persons acquiring their new but obviously short-lived freedom shows that more than 90 per cent of the divorcees marry again.

A more detailed analysis of the available statistics indicates

[7] Rubinow, "Marriage Rate Increasing in Spite of Divorce," *Current History Magazine*, November, 1928, pp. 289-294.

REMARRIAGE

that from 35 to 40 per cent of divorced people marry again within one year of the divorce. Between 60 and 65 per cent have married again within five years from the time of the divorce, and nearly 80 per cent within ten years.

The conclusion is inevitable that 'what comes after divorce' is frequently taken into consideration before the divorce is asked for.[9]

From 1928 to 1930 Dr. Rubinow has raised his estimate of the total percentage of American divorced persons remarrying, excluding those who die soon after divorce, from 80 per cent to 90 per cent. This viewpoint seemingly is that almost every divorce makes four people happy!

Dr. Rubinow analyzed the divorces granted for the decade 1910-1919 inclusive in elaborate detail in a previous article.[10] He accepted the decennial census figures on divorced population without challenge. His calculations were about as follows: 341,000 divorced persons were living in the United States in 1910; 2,112,000 additional divorcees were created by decrees granted during the years 1910-1919, inclusive, making a total of 2,453,000 divorced persons in the United States for 1920 if none had died or remarried. He estimated that according to the normal death rate of adults, about 150,000 died during this period, leaving 2,303,000 divorced persons alive who either remained divorced or had remarried. The 1920 decennial census listed only 509,000 divorced persons. Dr. Rubinow subtracted this figure from the 2,203,-000 divorced persons alive, and found a mysterious balance, according to his phraseology, of 1,794,000. He concluded that this number had remarried during that decade. Thus he summarized that 6 per cent of the divorcees died, 17 per cent remained divorced and 77 per cent remarried. Elimi-

[9] Rubinow, "After Divorce, What?" *New Republic*, July 16, 1930, p. 228.

[10] Rubinow, "Marriage Rate Increasing in Spite of Divorces," *Current History Magazine*, November, 1928, pp. 289-294.

104 *STATISTICAL ANALYSIS OF AMERICAN DIVORCE*

nating those who died, five out of six divorced persons remarried according to his estimate.

He advanced his theory so far as to speculate that of the
10,000,000 marriages, from 1909-1919 inclusive, probably
about 2,000,000 were contributed by remarrying divorced
parties. An 80 or 90 per cent remarriage of divorced people
is certainly a sensational figure. If Dr. Rubinow's estimate
is correct, then one-fifth of all marriage licenses go to former
divorced people, indicating a state either of progressive mon-
ogamy or polygamy on the installment plan.

This interesting calculation of Dr. Rubinow presents two
plain difficulties. The first one, not so serious, is the under-
estimation of the death rate of divorced persons. He assumes that they die at about the same proportion as the general adult population. Professor Willcox, after investigation, discovered that the death rate of divorcees is far higher
than that of married persons, and is equal to that of widowed
persons, although the widowed are considerably older than
divorcees [11] Dr. Dike, many years ago, found likewise
Since the death rate of divorcees is considerably higher than
that of the average adult population, the number of divorced
persons dying during the 1910-1919 period was somewhat
underestimated by Dr. Rubinow; but this is not a grave
error.

The serious mistake is that Dr. Rubinow never challenged
the crude decennial census figure for the number of divorced
persons. Here follows a quotation from the editor of the
decennial census for 1910:

It seems practically certain that the census returns as to the
number of divorced persons not remarried are far below the
true total. Some divorced persons have been reported as
single, married or widowed. If the number of persons reported
as divorced in 1910 is correct, the average length of time elaps-

[11] *New York State Department of Health Annual Report*, 1912, p. 244.

REMARRIAGE

ing between divorce and remarriage or death would be only 2.0 years. It seems incredible that this should be the case, and it is probable that the number of persons recorded as divorced in 1910 was considerably less than the actual number.[12]

Dr. Rubinow ignored the advice of both 1910 and 1920 census editors. Consequently, the small figure of 509,000 divorced persons listed in 1920 appeared to him to indicate that all the rest had remarried, therefore giving this mysterious balance of 1,794,000.

As previously shown for 1920, the time elapsing between divorce and either death or remarriage would necessarily be only one year and ten months if the decennial census figure of 509,000 is not underestimated. Even Dr. Rubinow would not admit remarriage is that hasty, since his 1930 article in the *New Republic* reckons that about 35 to 40 per cent of divorced people marry again within one year of divorce and between 60 and 65 per cent have married again within five years from the time of the divorce. Consequently there is an inconsistency between his reasoning and the decennial census figures upon which his conclusions are based. One need not further emphasize the census underestimate of divorced persons. Obviously an accurate estimate would greatly increase the number of divorced persons remaining divorced with a corresponding decrease of the percentage estimated as remarrying. The crucial point is to discover some constructive index that tells to how large a degree the decennial census underestimates the number of divorced people living in the United States.

Strangely the only source of information is the last government report on prisoners, which classifies the marital status of a sample of 18,000 men committed to state and federal penitentiaries.[13] The percentage of these men listed

[12] *U S. Census*, 1910, vol. i, pp. 507-508.

[13] U. S. Census, *Prisoners 1923* (Washington, 1926), pp. 82-83.

106 *STATISTICAL ANALYSIS OF AMERICAN DIVORCE*

as divorced is 2 7 of the total number. The average percentage divorced in the under-estimated decennial census for the entire male population over 15 years of age is .6.[14] The prison census enumerators are probably more accurate in obtaining information on marital status. Prisoners would not be so ashamed to admit divorces, and the statements of prisoners can be checked pretty accurately from the past records of inmates.

The editor of this prison report states:

The high percentage of divorced prisoners probably represents in large part a result of their arrest and conviction for former offenses, since the laws of many states list conviction for felony or imprisonment in the penitentiary as grounds for divorce. There were 810 divorces in the year 1923 recorded as due to these causes.

At the same time it should be noted that the number of divorced persons as reported in the general population census is believed to be seriously deficient. The reported number of divorced prisoners may have been somewhat more complete than the general population figures, in which case the exceptionally high ratio of divorced prisoners may be somewhat larger than the true ratios.[15]

Evidently the percentage of divorced persons among the prison population cannot be an accurate sample of the general American population without some corrections. Other factors influence these respective divorce rates. Almost all states allow divorces on the ground of felony or imprisonment. Consequently, this would make the divorce rate of prisoners abnormally high if many persons were divorced on that ground, which does not happen to be the case.

For the year 1923 there were 329,000 men committed to prison.[16] Over 800 were divorced that year upon the ground

[14] *U. S. Census*, 1920, vol. ii, p. 390.

[15] U. S. Census, *Prisoners 1923*, p. 83.

[16] *Ibid.*, p. 46.

REMARRIAGE

of felony or imprisonment. A correction for this factor reduces the percentage of divorced men in the prison population from 2.7 to 2.4. The latter figure is four times the percentage of males divorced in the general adult population. This still leaves a problem whether there is any proclivity of divorced men toward penitentiaries. If one assumed from Dr. Rubinow's estimate that over five-sixths of the people who had once been divorced have now remarried, this would be of no particular difficulty. It would have been simple for divorced men to remarry before they entered prisons. Since the rate was corrected for the number of men, divorced by their wives after they had entered prisons, there seems no other attraction between divorced men who had not remarried and penitentiaries. Accordingly, the 2.4 percentage of divorced men in prisons tends to be a fairly normal estimate because divorced men in prisons are unable to conceal their marital status as males of the general population do Consequently, here is a census report from which to measure the admitted inadequacy of the decennial census figure for 1920. The 1923 prison report thus shows there is four times the percentage of divorced men given by the decennial census. On this assumption four times as many divorced persons are extant as are listed in the decennial census report. This would bring the divorced population into a closer numerical relationship with the increasing number of divorces yearly granted.

One must reëxamine the figures for divorce and divorcees for the decade from 1910-1919 inclusive. The same method of calculation is used as that of Dr. Rubinow because it applied very well with two decided exceptions. He underestimated the deaths of divorcees, and he assumed as correct the admittedly inadequate decennial census estimate of the number of divorced persons alive. The first step is to quadruple the number of divorcees listed alive at the time of the

108 STATISTICAL ANALYSIS OF AMERICAN DIVORCE

1910 census. This would give a figure of 1,364,000. To this are added as before 2,112,000 persons who were divorced during the ten-year period. These combined figures give a total for the year 1920 of 3,476,000 persons once divorced, who were at that time either dead, remarried or still divorced. The next step is to subtract the number who died. Dr. Rubinow's figure of 6 per cent was inadequate for reasons hitherto expressed. Probably any selected figure will not be high enough to represent the number of divorcees who died because the death rate of divorcees is estimated to be higher than that of married persons for the same ages. The death rate in that decade for all persons over the age of 15 represented about 10 per cent fatality.[17] For divorced persons alone the death rate would be at least that high. Thus there can be subtracted 348,000 deaths from the previous 1920 figure, leaving 3,128,000 divorced persons who remained divorced or who had remarried by 1920. Now if the underestimated 1920 divorced population is quadrupled, this gives a figure of 2,036,000 persons who remained divorced. After this latter is subtracted from the total, one finds that 1,092,000 persons divorced had remarried in that decade. To recapitulate, this computation shows that at least 10 per cent died, 31 per cent remarried, and 58 per cent of the divorced population remained under the category of divorced. After divorcees who die are excluded, one finds that only 35 per cent of divorced persons remarry.

Additional information is provided by a press release of the 1930 census.[18] It lists the number of divorced persons as 1,063,000, an increase of 109 per cent over 1920. The 1920-1929 decade showed an increase in divorces granted of only 66 per cent over the 1910-1919 decade. Thus the increase of divorced persons in the 1930 census is dispropor-

---

[17] U. S. Life Tables, 1910 (Washington, 1921), p. 51.

[18] U. S. Census, press release 7 on population, Aug. 31, 1931.

REMARRIAGE

tionately high. Only three factors can account for this. The first, a substantial decrease in the death rate of divorcees, is scarcely plausible. The second, a decline in the remarriage rate of divorced persons, would be dependent on a change in human nature and therefore a difficult explanation to believe. The third factor means a more complete enumeration of divorced persons in 1930 than in the 1920 census. This can be attributed to a change in the mores represented by a growing social approval of divorce, so that a greater proportion of divorced persons was willing to admit being divorced when questioned by census enumerators as to marital status; thus confirming the conclusion heretofore stated.

A sensational explanation of divorce attributed primarily to remarriage cannot be supported by the facts. An estimate of one-third remarriage of divorced persons, derived from secondary statistical sources, corroborates the previously cited opinions of experts and a few scattered state figures. It must be remembered that widowed persons remarry Many of the divorcees constituting the one-third who rewed probably had no idea of remarriage at the time of the divorce suit.[19] There is no evidence that increasing desire for remarriage has been a substantial cause of the fivefold advance of the American divorce rate during the past six decades.

The preceding three chapters have examined three popular ideas as to the causes of divorce, and have ascertained that migratory divorce, marriage and divorce legislation, and remarriage are not effective causes of increasing divorce The remaining chapters treat the diminishing size of the family, the shortening duration of marriage, and persistent economic trends operating upon American family breakdown, as tangible causes of increasing divorce.

---

[19] The psychological state of mind as to the intent of remarriage, among divorce applicants at the time of suit, cannot be estimated. The foregoing figures simply give an approximation as to the extent of remarriage.

CHAPTER VIII

TRENDS OF THE VANISHING FAMILY

THE diminishing number of children and the shortening duration of married life in broken homes are two trends associated with the declining cohesiveness of the American family. The modern custom of fewer children undermines a traditional function of the family and removes one of the chief factors binding the activities of the household together. Professor Charles A. Ellwood of the University of Missouri discussed the vanishing American home in an article entitled " Is the American Family to Die? " A quotation follows:

Statistics prove that it is the most vital question before the American public today. The family is the most important institution of human society. It is the function of the family in society to conserve all social possessions and hand them down to the next generation. Not only are the material possessions thus preserved, but also the spiritual possessions of the race— language, religion, art, morality, government and ideals. The family thus preserves the social continuity from one generation to another; it reproduces not only the new individuals of each generation but also society itself. Moreover, in the relations of the members of the family to each other we have the source of altruism upon which society depends for each upward advance; hence moral progress in society rests upon the family.[1]

As is well known, the birth rate in the United States has been steadily declining.[2] For 1915 the rate was 25.1 per

[1] Ellwood 'Is the American Family to Die?" *Delineator*, February, 1909, pp. 228-229.

[2] *U. S. Birth, Stillbirth and Infant Mortality Statistics*, 1929, mimeographed material.

TRENDS OF THE VANISHING FAMILY

Percent of Divorces Involving Children, 1928

CHART 11

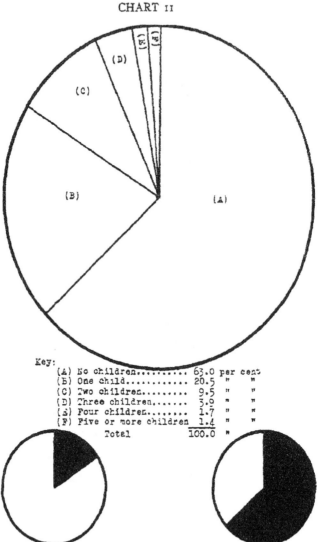

Key:
(A) No children.......... 63.0 per cent
(B) One child............ 20.5 "   "
(C) Two children......... 9.5   "   "
(D) Three children....... 3.9   "   "
(E) Four children........ 1.7   "   "
(F) Five or more children 1.4   "   "
　　　　Total   100.0 "

■ Childless Marriages, 16%　　■ Childless Divorces, 63%

112 STATISTICAL ANALYSIS OF AMERICAN DIVORCE

thousand population, while in 1929 the birth rate has declined to 18.9. During the same fifteen-year period divorces in this country increased from 2.65 to 4.05 per thousand married population. Professor Ogburn correlated divorced persons with birth rates of 170 cities, a partial correlation holding age of wife constant, and obtained a coefficient — 54, indicating a marked negative association between the birth rate and the divorce rate.[3]

This relation is particularly significant to divorce as Chart 11 shows by the large circle diagram, the respective percentages of divorced families classified according to the number of children affected. The distribution for 1928 follows:

TABLE 7. PERCENTAGE DISTRIBUTION OF DIVORCES ACCORDING TO SIZE OF FAMILY, 1928

No children .	.	..	..	.	63 0
One child . .	.	.	.	. . .	20 5
Two children . . .	.	. .	.	.	9 5
Three children			.	. .	3 9
Four children . . .	.	. . . .	.		1 7
Five or more	. .	. . .	. .		1.4

Total 100

Expressing the relation in a more definite form, one notes that as children increase arithmetically divorce corresponding decreases at a geometrical rate; in other words, the more children the less divorce.

Almost two thirds of divorces come from the childless married population. Has such childlessness materially increased and therefore provided a larger relative percentage of the population from which to draw potential divorces? From Massachusetts figures Dr. Willcox in 1891 estimated that about 18 per cent of the families were childless.[4] Dr.

[3] Groves and Ogburn, *American Marriage and Family Relationships*, p. 378.

[4] Willcox, *The Divorce Problem, a Study in Statistics*, p. 19.

TRENDS OF THE VANISHING FAMILY 113

Alfred J. Lotka of the Metropolitan Life Insurance Company recently estimated by refined mathematical calculations that about 17 per cent of American marriages are sterile, or just a trifle higher proportion of childless marriages, than the approximation given by Dr. Willcox over forty years ago.[5]

Chart 12 presents circle diagrams on the chances of divorce. As previously stated, American marriages show about an 18 per cent fatality in the divorce court. Simple arithmetic computations show that 71 per cent of childless marriages in America end in divorce, while only 8 per cent of married couples with children eventually are divorced.[6]

Journalists frequently arouse sympathy for the ill-fated children of divorced parents. The annual quota of such children is less than one-third the number of divorced persons, but they may attract newspaper publicity. Only about 7 per cent of American divorces are granted to couples with three or more children while three is traditionally the normal American family quota. Ferris F. Laune, Executive Secretary of the Wieboldt Foundation, stated: " A study of parental status of 4,100 children in thirty-one public homes was made in 1923. The results show that 25 per cent of these children came from homes broken by separation or divorce." [7]

Dr. George L. Koehn of Reed College surveyed homeless children in Portland, Oregon, as related to divorced parents.[8]

[5] Lotka, " Sterility in American Marriage," *Proceedings of the National Academy of Sciences*, January, 1928, pp. 99-109

[6] Sixty-three per cent of the divorces come from about one-sixth or 17 per cent of the marriages, the sterile ones. If all marriages were sterile, the probability of divorce would be 63 per cent of the present divorce rate multiplied by six.

[7] Mowrer, *Domestic Discord* (Chicago, 1928), foreword by Ferris F. Laune.

[8] Koehn, " Is Divorce a Social Menace? " *Current History Magazine*, May, 1922, pp. 294-299.

CHART 12

PROBABILITIES OF DIVORCE ACCORDING TO PRESENCE OR ABSENCE OF CHILDREN, 1928

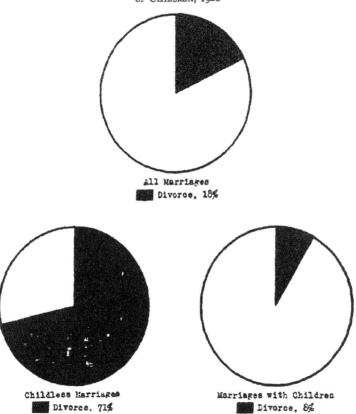

All Marriages
■ Divorce, 18%

Childless Marriages
■ Divorce, 71%

Marriages with Children
■ Divorce, 8%

Portland for many years has been the highest divorce producing city among localities of over 100,000 population in this country, averaging more than one divorce for every two marriages. It must be recalled that almost two-thirds of the divorces are granted to childless couples, and of the remaining percentage less than two children is the average per couple. Consequently, the actual number of children of

TRENDS OF THE VANISHING FAMILY   115

divorced parents would be relatively small to the total children in a city. The results for Portland indicated the following anti-social effects of divorce by the percentages of abandoned children from broken homes.

TABLE 8.   DIVORCE AND HOMELESS CHILDREN IN PORTLAND, OREGON, 1921

Institution	Percent
Boys' and Girls' Aid Society	18
Florence Crittenden Refuge Home	18
House of Good Shepherd	31
Salvation Army Rescue and Maternity Home	33
Christy House for Orphan Girls	35
Pacific Coast Rescue and Protective Society	36
Oregon State Industrial School for Girls	59

The substance of this brief section can be stated that divorce is not a universal American family habit since almost two-thirds of the divorces are recruited from the 17 per cent childless marriages, and an additional 20 per cent of the divorces or the majority of the remainder, come from that comparatively small category, the one-child marriage. Sterility in marriage appears not to have changed in this country during the past few decades. However, the diminishing size of the family and its declining cohesiveness are noted by the correspondence of the decreasing birth rate to the increasing divorce rate. Professor Ogburn found a higher degree of association between divorce and birth rates of cities than between any other factors correlated. Finally the inverse relationship between the number of offspring in the home and the probabilities of divorce strongly suggests a causal connection here. The astonishing 71 per cent fatality of childless American marriages indicates a dismally low chance of success for marital happiness where children do not force the preservation of the home.

The shortening duration of marriages, where divorces eventually occur, is likewise of growing importance in the

116 STATISTICAL ANALYSIS OF AMERICAN DIVORCE

investigation of causes of increasing American divorce.   The advance of the divorce rate has been paralleled by constantly briefer periods of married life before the home is severed. Prior to the statement of this relationship between increasing divorce and the shortening duration of marriage, there follows a detailed analysis of the relative probabilities of divorce according to the different years of married life.

Three methods are employed for computing the probability of an average marriage ending in divorce.   The first is popularly used in comparing the number of divorces annually with the number of marriages   This is erroneous because no logical relationship exists between the two.   Very few people are divorced the same year they are married; in fact, the median average lag between marriage and divorce among those marriages eventually destined to end in divorce is about seven years.   Consequently, a ratio between marriages and divorces of the same year under-estimates the chances of divorce.

Another method of calculating the chances of divorce is a comparison of the number of divorces annually with the number of deaths of married persons, since all marriages are eventually broken by one or the other.   This is likewise erroneous, for again there is no logical relationship between the two.   Since the people who are being divorced at the present time are much younger than the majority of those who are dying, this method is actually comparing current divorces with deaths of several years ago if the age factor were held constant, and consequently over-estimates the chances of divorce.

A correct method for estimating the probability of divorce requires more refined computations.   One must follow the course of marriages contracted, and ascertain what proportion of the total ends in divorce for each year of married life. Chart 13 is a frequency curve showing the relative percent-

CHART 13

PERCENTAGE DISTRIBUTION OF DIVORCES GRANTED IN 1928 FOR FIRST THIRTY YEARS OF MARRIAGE

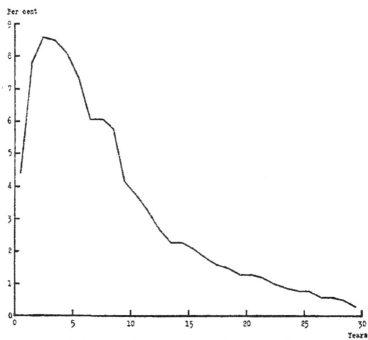

ages of divorce by given years of marriage, for the first thirty years of married life, as given in the 1928 *U. S. Marriage and Divorce Report*. Only about 2 per cent of the divorces occur after the thirtieth year of marriage. About half of the divorces occur during the first seven years. Inspection of the graph shows that the mode, which is the year of marriage with the highest number of divorces, falls during the third year of married life. There is a rapid rise in divorces virtually from the wedding day until the third year of marriage, and then commences a slow and steady decline in divorce frequency. The abnormally low percentage of divorces

118 STATISTICAL ANALYSIS OF AMERICAN DIVORCE

in the sixth year was merely due to an excessive number of marriages in 1922.

The *U. S. Marriage and Divorce Report* for 1928 also distributes the total number of divorces by years of marriage, such as 1928, 1915, 1899 or any other year. If the number of divorces in each of these annual intervals is divided into the number of marriages for each of these years respectively, one finds the yearly percentages of marriages that end in divorce Thus a new frequency table is constructed for the probability of divorce in each year of married life. Of 10,000 couples 1,792 would eventually end in divorce, or about 18 per cent, according to the 1928 rate of divorce in the United States. This final figure was obtained by adding the percentages of divorces occurring for each of the first thirty years of marriage. This was corrected for certain minor factors The divorces occurring after the thirtieth year of marriage were based upon the thirty-fifth year and a percentage calculated. Since over 4,000 marriages were annulled in 1928 these were based upon the second year, the median for annulment, and a percentage likewise calculated. Finally a miscellaneous class of divorces totaling 11,000 was recorded but without knowledge of the year in which marriage took place, and to this number were added about 500 estimated divorces to Americans given by the foreign decrees. From this sub-total were subtracted about 6,000 divorces, as a recent government divorce report has shown that about this percentage of divorces is annually granted to persons living in the United States who had been married in foreign countries. The miscellaneous figure remaining was based at the seventh year of marriage, the median for divorce, and a percentage was likewise calculated. All the percentage estimates for the thirty years of married life plus all the corrections for minor factors were totalled; giving the summation frequency of 17.92, or about 18 per cent, which is the probability of an American marriage ending in divorce for the last available year, 1928.[1]

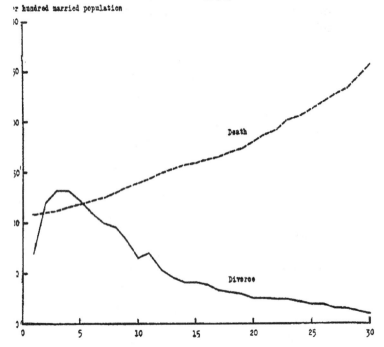

CHART 14

RELATIVE PROBABILITIES OF DIVORCE AND DEATH FOR FIRST THIRTY YEARS OF MARRIAGE, 1928

Chart 14 presents this data in a frequency curve for the probabilities of marriage being ended by divorce for each year of married life The first year shows that 70 couples in every 10,000 will resort to the divorce courts. The second year lists 120, or 1.2 per cent. The third and fourth years are modal, each having 1 32 per cent as broken by di-

[1] This estimate refers to divorces occurring in 1928, the marriages being distributed over a period of more than thirty preceding years Future probability estimates are based on this past experience.

120 *STATISTICAL ANALYSIS OF AMERICAN DIVORCE*

TABLE 9 DIVORCE IN RELATION TO DURATION OF MARRIAGE, 1928

Years of Married Life	Divorces per Hundred Married Population	Death of Spouse per Hundred Married Population	Adjusted Divorce Frequency
1	70	1.08	.71
2	I 20	1.10	I 23
3	1.32	I 12	I 37
4	I 32	I 16	1.38
5	1.27	1.18	I 35
6	I 10	1.22	I 18
7	I 00	1.26	I 09
8	.97	1.30	I 07
9	.84	1.36	94
10	.67	1.40	.76
11	72	1.44	.83
12	54	1.50	64
13	47	1.54	.56
14	.42	1.58	51
15	.42	1.60	.52
16	.39	1.64	.50
17	.34	1.68	44
18	.32	1.72	43
19	30	I 76	.41
20	.26	1.82	36
21	26	1.90	.37
22	.24	1.94	.35
23	.24	2 04	.37
24	22	2.08	.35
25	.19	2 16	.31
26	19	2 22	.32
27	.16	2.30	.28
28	.15	2.36	.28
29	.13	2 48	.25
30	.10	2.60	.20

vorce. The abnormally high frequency for the eleventh year
is due to war marriages, even a decade later. The thirtieth
year of marriage lists only .10 per cent. This graph is more
accurate than the previous frequency curve because it takes
account of the increasing number of marriages in recent
years. Since the number of marriages in this country has

TRENDS OF THE VANISHING FAMILY

been rising for many years, divorces occurring during the early years of life would be more frequent for that reason. Chart 14 eliminates this biasing factor, and consequently is less skewed toward the later years of married life. Although it is true that the majority of divorces take place during the early years of married life, unrefined figures are likely to exaggerate this idea. The previous Chart 13 is based entirely on the unmodified percentages given in the government divorce report. The mode there was in the third year of marriage. After the data has been refined to account for the increasing number of marriages within recent years and therefore a larger number of married people who could potentially be divorced, the modal year then passes to a position exactly placed between the third and fourth years. Another reason to be considered for more divorces occurring in early married life is because a greater percentage of the spouses are still alive to be divorced, while in later years death has taken an increasingly large toll with consequently a fewer number left for the divorce courts. The dotted line in Chart 14 shows a calculated death rate per hundred married population during each year of wedded life.

This refinement was obtained by assuming that the majority of persons eventually to be married have wedded by their twenty-fourth year of life, as given in the decennial census figures for 1920.[9] The death rates for each year of age were applied after the twenty-fourth year.[10] These yearly death rates were doubled to allow for marital rather than individual death rates, since the death of either spouse would dissolve a marriage. The derived figures are shown by the dotted line in Chart 14, which is a rough estimate of the probabilities of dissolution by death for each year of married life. Thus during the first five years of marriage divorce outranks

[9] *U. S. Census*, 1920, vol. ii, pp. 391-392.
[10] *U. S. Life Tables*, 1910, p. 54.

CHART 15

CORRECTED DISTRIBUTION SHOWING PROBABILITIES OF DIVORCE FOR FIRST THIRTY YEARS OF MARRIAGE, 1928

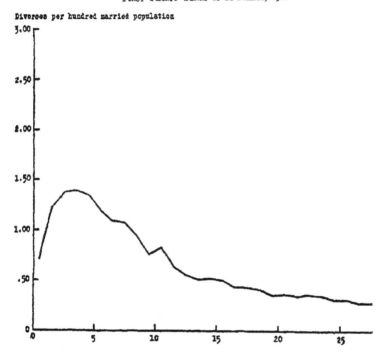

death as a breaker of the American home. After that death steadily increases while divorce speedily declines during the later years of married life.

A new table of the probabilities of divorce by years of marriage was constructed on the basis of this refined data which take into account both the marriage rate and the death rate. The purpose is to ascertain the probabilities of divorce by years of marriage after corrections have been made for the increasing number of deaths during the later years of married life This frequency curve, Chart 15, is much less skewed

TRENDS OF THE VANISHING FAMILY   123

than its two predecessors. The mode has now passed definitely to the fourth year of marriage, and the chance of divorce in the thirtieth year of marriage is twice as high as that shown in the previous frequency curve. This chart takes account of the fact that less couples are still alive in the later years of married life, with the possibilities of divorce to face them.

Parallel to the trend of increasing American divorce for the past six decades is the increasing popularity of divorce during the earlier years of marriage. In the first *U. S. Marriage and Divorce Report,* 1867-1886, the mode for divorce fell during the seventh year of marriage. For the second period, 1887-1906, the modal year of divorce was the fifth of married life. From 1922-1928 the annual marriage and divorce reports show that the modal year has fallen still lower, now fluctuating between the third and fourth years of marriage.

A comparison of the states for the year 1928 demonstrates this high correspondence between early divorce and high divorce rates. Of the forty-eight states, twenty-five have the modal year of divorce during the third or fourth year of married life, which is the same as the national average. In twelve states the modal year of divorce occurs during the fifth of married life. These are: California, Connecticut, Delaware, the District of Columbia, Maine, Maryland, Massachusetts, New Jersey, New York, Virginia, Vermont and West Virginia. All these states, with the exception of California, are conservative divorce states, and incidentally, Atlantic Seaboard states. Lowness of divorce rates and tardiness of suits correspond here similarly.

The following states fall below the modal year for the country and grant divorces in the second year of married life at the highest frequency: Arizona, Arkansas, Idaho, Indiana, Kansas, Missouri, Ohio, Oklahoma, Oregon, Nevada and

CHART 16

LENGTH OF MARRIED LIFE TILL DEATH OR DIVORCE, 1928

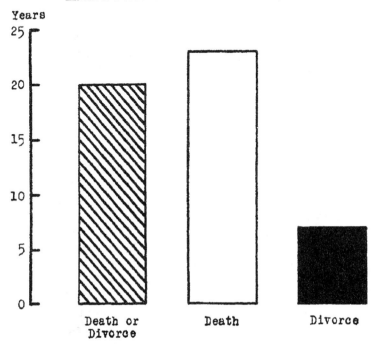

Wyoming. All eleven of these states rank very high in divorce rates including the four leaders. High rates and earliness of divorce are shown to be in striking correspondence.

The shortness of married life in the divorced family contrasted to the unbroken home is particularly marked The median average between marriage and divorce is about seven years. What is the length of ordinary American marriage? A crude estimate of this can be computed by striking an average for the number of American marriages for three years centered at 1928. If one then divides the total number of married couples living in the United States by the

TRENDS OF THE VANISHING FAMILY   125

total marriages for the same year, this gives a rough approximation of the length of American marriages, specifically, 20.4 years till death or divorce shall part as shown in Chart 16.

Since 18 per cent of the marriages end in divorce at an average of 7 years' duration, these reduce the length of married life 13.4 years times 18 per cent, or 2.4 years. Addition of this latter figure to the average length of marriage (20.4 years) tells that about 23 years is the length of an American marriage till death removes either spouse, if divorce were non-existent.

The foregoing facts and illustrations indicate the relatively high probabilities of divorce during the early years of married life, even after corrections are allowed for both the marriage rate and the death rate. This tendency toward earlier divorces is numerically marked, parallel to the increase of the total American divorce rate during the past six decades. This relationship is further accentuated by the correspondence between high divorce rates and early divorces in the states. The first section of the chapter concerned with the diminishing size of the family and this part dealing with shortening duration of marriages that terminate in divorce both present clear indices of family disintegration, factors leading to a final analysis of causes of increasing divorce.

CHAPTER IX

Persistent Causes

Economic and social changes have occurred with unbelievable rapidity in the entire development of American life during the last six decades. The influence of these fundamental changes as persistent, long-time factors in family breakdown is of primary concern What are the causes of increasing American divorce, which are measurable statistically, that have effected a fivefold advancement of the national divorce rate from 1867 to the present day? First will be examined some basic reasons for increasing divorce as expounded by expert students of this problem.

Professor Walter F. Willcox of Cornell University has written more extensively on the subject of American divorce statistics over a period of forty .years than any other authority. Recently he summarized the principal causes of increasing divorce [1] One factor of importance is the greater proportion of persons in the community who have an income sufficient to pay the requisite legal fee. Another, the change in the mores and public opinion toward divorce corresponding to the growth of individualism and the frank recognition that the happiness of parties concerned is of dominant importance. A third is the declining belief in the family as an institution ordained by God and a weakening of religious attitudes toward marriage in the United States.

Professor William F. Ogburn of the University of Chicago wrote a few years ago as follows:

[1] Willcox, " Divorce in the U. S.," *Encyclopedia Britannica*, vol. viii, pp. 459-460.

PERSISTENT CAUSES

Court records give us little information about the more fundamental causes of divorce that lie deep in the nature of society or in human nature. Many basic causes are found in the decline in various functions of the family. The family used to be the economic unit in the older agricultural society, but now these services have passed to the state, the factory, the restaurant and the store. The protective function has passed in large measures to the state, the courts, the school, the health boards and so forth. Recreation is still a home affair to a slight extent, but it has become largely commercialized. The religious function has largely passed from the home, due to changes in the nature of religious beliefs and creeds. The school is taking younger and younger children and there are fewer and fewer of them. The loss of these functions continues. They were bonds or ties that helped to keep members of the family together.[2]

Professor James P. Lichtenberger of the University of Pennsylvania investigated this subject almost two decades ago, and arrived at conclusions not much different from the recent summaries of Professors Willcox and Ogburn. Dr. Lichtenberger divided the great changes in American development since the Civil War into social, religious and economic categories. Under the classification of social liberation, he listed the growth of individualism and the increasing liberty of American women. The religious category included the passing of dogmatism and revised ethical concepts of the family. Dr. Lichtenberger's poignant summary of the influences of economic changes in America upon the increasing divorce rate deserves repetition:

The period of most rapid modern-industrial development in the United States practically coincides with the period of the rapid increase of the divorce rate. This phenomena is sufficient to furnish a presumption in favor of a close correlation if not a

---

[2] Groves and Ogburn, *American Marriage and Family Relationships*, p. 128.

128 STATISTICAL ANALYSIS OF AMERICAN DIVORCE

positive relation of cause and effect. One of the most significant results of our modern economic progress is the increasing
strain it lays upon the individual through the maladjustment
which it inevitably creates. While economic progress ultimately means the increased well-being of society, it intensifies
the selective process by which it is attained, and social wreckage
strews the path of advance. This is illustrated in the phenomena of increasing insanity, suicide and crime. These bear
a direct ratio to the degree of civilization attained. They are
the social costs of progress, and the higher the rate of progress
the greater is the burden on society that these costs impose.
The more rapid the advance of the army, the more numerous
are the men who fall out of the ranks. The number of divorces
has steadily risen with the increase of progress and the growth
of civilization. Conditions of life, which strain the mental and
nervous constitution to the breaking point, are destined in multiplied instances to result in discord within the domestic circle
and thus increase the probabilities of divorce.[3]

The leading authorities on American divorce thus believe
that its increase is inextricably interwoven with the social,
religious and economic phases in the development of advancing material progress in this country. The outstanding
points in their summaries fall in two categories, those factors
capable of quantitative treatment and other forces not
directly measurable.

An endeavor will here be made to compare the figures
given in various statistical indices showing the trends of
different economic and social series with the trend of the divorce rate. Certain probable causes of increasing divorce,
such as growing social degeneracy represented by crime and
insanity, declining religious influence, the rise of individualism, and changing public attitude toward divorce must be
set aside till the final chapter as ineligible material for the
present numerical comparisons.

[3] Lichtenberger, *Divorce a Study in Social Causation*, pp. 155-156.

PERSISTENT CAUSES

The primary interest is the examination of concomitant, measurable factors to elucidate positive causes of increasing divorce or to refute fallacious ideas on the problem. Both by a priori reasoning and cited authorities, four important factors, contributing to increasing divorce, which are directly measuarable, may be assumed to be represented by the following:

1. The rise of economic production.
2. The growth of cities.
3. The increase of women wage-earners.
4. The declining birth rate.

Unfortunately, exact data concerning these series is somewhat lacking, so the derived estimates are less accurate than divorce rates. Since yearly information was not available for three of the series, it was necessary to use decennial figures.

Thus there are only seven items for each respective series: namely, 1870, 1880, 1890, 1900, 1910, 1920 and 1930. Divorce rate figures required liberal adjustments. Although the number of divorces for each year was available, rates had not been computed on the basis of divorces per thousand married population for the early years. This required interpolation in order to obtain intercensal estimates of the annual married population; then divorce rates were calculated for the early period from the divorce figures, which had always been given by the government reports on an annual basis. Nine year averages were centered to obtain decennial estimates for divorces per thousand married population, except for the first and last figures.

The index of economic production here employed was that of eighty-seven commodities of industrial, agricultural and miscellaneous variety compiled by Carl Snyder for the years

130 *STATISTICAL ANALYSIS OF AMERICAN DIVORCE*

1870 to 1930 inclusive.[4]   Nine year averages were centered for decennial estimates.

Decennial figures for the percentage of the total population living in cities of more than 8,000 people were obtained from a census monograph by Dr. Leon E. Truesdell.[5]   Data for the percentage of gainfully employed women over the age of sixteen was secured from a census monograph by Dr. Joseph A. Hill.[6]   Figures for 1930 on urban growth [7] and women wage-earners [8] were adjusted from data given in the recent census.

A substitute for decennial birthrates was suggested a couple of decades ago by Professor Willcox.[9]   This consisted simply of the number of children under five years of age per thousand women between the ages of fifteen and forty-four, as given in every decennial census.

TABLE 10. TRENDS OF DIVORCE AND FOUR RELATED ECONOMIC AND SOCIAL FACTORS

Year	Divorce Rate	Economic Production	Urban Growth	Ratio of Children	Women Workers
1870	82	33 80	20.9	620	14.7
1880	1 07	44.30	22 7	609	16.0
1890	1.40	48.47	29 0	529	19.0
1900	1 83	65.77	32 9	518	20.6
1910	2 40	94 97	38.7	488	23 7
1920	3 14	128.55	43 8	467	24.0
1930	3.65	148 42	49 1	391	25 1

[4] Snyder, *Business Cycles and Business Measurements* (New York, 1927), p. 239. This index was continued 1925 to 1931 in the January issues of *Monthly Review of Credit and Business Conditions*, Second Federal Reserve District.

[5] Truesdell, *Farm Population in the United States* (Washington, 1926), p 24.

[6] Hill, *Women in Gainful Occupations, 1870-1920* (Washington, 1929), p. 19. 1910 figure was adjusted according to Dr. Hill's reasons, ch. iii.

[7] *U. S. Census*, 1930, vol. i, p 9.

[8] *U. S. Census*, press release 10 on population, Sept. 9, 1931.

[9] Willcox, "The Change in the Proportion of Children in the U. S.," *Quarterly Publications of the American Statistical Association*, March, 1911, pp. 490-499.

CHART 17
Growth of Divorce and Four Related Factors on Ratio Scale

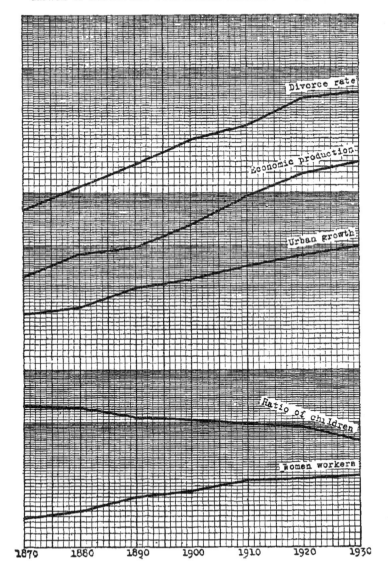

132 STATISTICAL ANALYSIS OF AMERICAN DIVORCE

Decennial figures for these five series constitute the only available material for a comparison of trends. Admittedly there are errors in the data, but no reason appears for such to be biased or cumulative. Here the particular interest concerns the rates of change of divorce and of these four attendant factors The ratio chart, 17 shows the percentage increases of divorce and its four associated factors; namely, economic production, urban growth, women workers and the ratio of children. The lines of trend all portray influences in conformity with the rising divorce rate in the order of importance mentioned. Graphic presentation thus suggests apparent causes, the relative importance of which may be effected by the complication of interlocking relationships. Comparison of the divorce rate with these economic and social series indicates a complexity of interacting causes which makes difficult a final explanation of this problem in social causation. All of these factors seem associated and their influences are so blended with each other that it may be misleading to select the apparently outstanding factor, economic production, as the predominant cause of increasing divorce.

However, the economic interpretation of divorce will now be inspected more closely. It is both a popular and scientific belief that the divorce rate rises with prosperity and falls during business depression. Professor Willcox wrote recently:

The slight expense of obtaining a divorce is an important reason for the great number of decrees issued. The importance of this consideration is reflected in the fact that the divorce rate for the United States as a whole shows clearly in its fluctuations the influences of good and bad times. When times are good and the income of the working classes likely to be assured, the divorce rate rises. In periods of industrial depression it falls.[10]

[10] Willcox, " Divorce in the U. S ," *Encyclopedia Britannica*, vol. viii, p. 460.

PERSISTENT CAUSES

Dr. Joseph A. Hill of the United States Census Bureau has given the following reasons for the decrease of divorce in depression; (1) fewer marriages; (2) more sober living; (3) attorney's fees; (4) inability of wife to earn living.[11]

Dr Dorothy S. Thomas in an interesting experiment correlated the divorce rate in the United States with an index of business conditions compiled by herself and Professor Ogburn.[12] For the divorce rate she used the standard divorces per thousand population. As previously shown, a divorce rate based on the married population is the only one which will take into consideration the changes in the marriage rate. Since marriages decrease in depression more decidedly than do divorces, the standard employed may have an element of error. Dr. Thomas interpreted the positive correlation discovered between divorce and prosperity as follows:

> The tendency to secure more divorces in prosperity and fewer divorces in business depression is quite marked, and this conclusion is perhaps surprising. The reason is not clear, although the economic argument is clearer than the psychological. The fact that divorces are expensive, involving lawyers and court fees and perhaps alimony, may be the reason for relatively more divorce in times of business prosperity.[13]

The next step is to test this hypothesis, the relation between divorce and business cycles, as thoroughly as the statistical method may permit with the facts available. Divorce rates per thousand married population will be used for a sixty-year period, from 1870 to 1929 inclusive The composite index of economic production with which to compare

[11] Hill, " Statistics of Divorce," *Quarterly Publications of the American Statistical Association*, June, 1909, pp. 486-504.

[12] Thomas, *Social Aspects of the Business Cycle* (London, 1925), pp 64-67.

[13] *Ibid.*, p. 67.

CHART 18

ANNUAL FLUCTUATIONS IN RATES OF DIVORCE AND ECONOMIC
PRODUCTION ON RATIO SCALE

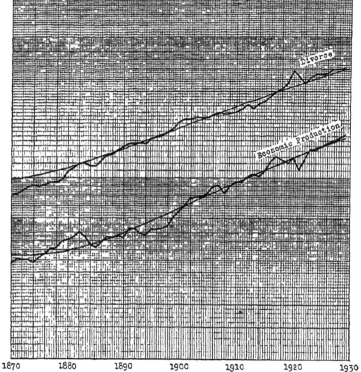

divorce rates will be that given by Carl Snyder, chief statistician of the Federal Reserve Bank of New York. He is quoted as follows:

The persistence and stability of growth of general production is further interesting because it is apparently independent of the growth of total population in this country The population rate of increase has been steadily declining through the past fifty years while the rate of growth of industrial production has

PERSISTENT CAUSES 135

remained constant. This is an indication of the steady expansion of the per capita production of the United States.[14]

Coincidentally, both divorce rates and economic production rates show a fivefold multiplication Second, degree parabolas were fitted to both of these long-time series, and thus the trends were removed as shown in ratio chart No. 18. This apparently leaves cyclical fluctuations of economic production and divorce rates.

After the trends have been removed, the correlation between these two time series shows a coefficient of only +.05. Allowing for a year lag of divorce rates behind economic production due to the slowness of court procedure, the coefficient of correlation still is merely +.07, seemingly showing a negligible association between fluctuations of divorce and the oscillations of business cycles.

This need not contradict the conclusion of writers, who have noticed a specific correspondence between lower divorce rates and business depressions. There were slight declines in the divorce rate during the same or following years of such major business depressions as 1875, 1884, 1894, 1908 and 1921. However, the divorce rate does not concur in the many years of periods of prosperity with either regularity or uniformity in correspondence to the fluctuations of business cycles. During the sixty-three year period the divorce rate per thousand married population declined only nine years.

TABLE II   YEARS OF DECLINING DIVORCE RATES

Year	Per cent	Year	Per cent
1872	2	1913	5
1875	2	1921	8
1884	3	1922	9 } 17
1894	2	1925	Negligible
1908	2		

[14] Snyder, *Business Cycles and Business Measurements*, p. 51.

136 STATISTICAL ANALYSIS OF AMERICAN DIVORCE

A press release on divorce figures for 1930, a year of financial depression, shows a substantial decrease in the divorce rate.[15]

The years of decline in the divorce rate have been few and, with the exception of the 17 per cent fall in 1921-1922, their amplitudes were small. Perhaps this one major decline was due to a normal readjustment after the inflated post-war divorce rate of 1919-1920. It is true that every year given as one of divorce decline occurred during or following a year of commercial depression or recession, as listed in a standard conspectus of business fluctuations [16] Perhaps low correlation coefficients between divorce and business conditions may be explained by the small reductions in the divorce rate contrasted to the severe collapse of economic production during the years of business panics. The above table shows divorce declines to be small in amplitude and short in duration, indicating slight abatements of increasing divorce during economic depression, probably on account of the costs of court actions.

This part of the inquiry has constituted an inductive approach to persistent causes of increasing divorce in the endeavor to explain the long and steady uniformity in the rise of the divorce rate for sixty-three years, advancing at a 3 per cent ratio of increment annually. The first stage in the process was a detailed survey of the causes of the increase given by experts Certain plausible causes stated by authorities were considered, but set aside as not now quantitatively measurable. Since this monograph is limited in scope, it can treat only those causes of increasing divorce which are estimable statistically; but, nevertheless, admits the existence of

---

[15] U. S. Census, *Preliminary Report on Marriage and Divorce for the United States: 1930*, July 23, 1931.

[16] Mitchell, *Business Cycles, the Problem and Its Setting* (New York, 1927), pp. 428-437.

PERSISTENT CAUSES

the operation of less tangible causes. The four principal, measurable factors; namely, economic production, urban growth, women workers and childlessness all have probably effected the phenomenon of rising divorce, but the importance of apparent causes is often misleading due to the complication of interacting influences. Finally, the hypothesis of economic determinism of divorce was tested by correlation of the divorce rate with business cycles and the very low degree of association indicates the fallacy of accepting an ostensible concurrence of factors as a causal relationship. American national home life is so diversified, and the changes in society of six decades so complex that a singular interpretation of increasing divorce is scarcely plausible. The four factors associated with the growth of divorce operate in the nature of concomitant or mutually interrelated forces, as chief environmental causes in American family breakdown.

CHAPTER X

Dynamic Society and Divorce Velocity

THIS study has considered the statistical evidence on divorce in the United States in relation to social and economic factors, showing the probability of divorce in American families The legal grounds alleged in divorce actions have been reviewed in contrast with the probable underlying causes; the relatively minor rôles played by migratory divorce, changing legislation, and desire to remarry have been analyzed; the trends of the decreasing size of the family and the shortening duration of marriage in broken homes have been related to the constantly increasing divorce rate. Finally, indices of changes in economic production over six decades, degrees of urbanization of the population, and increasing participation of women in the industrial life of the nation have been compared with the divorce rate, to show the profound transformations in a dynamic society to which the modern family must adjust itself.

A recapitulation of the trends, which may indicate some causes of increasing divorce, is now in order. The divorce rate has multiplied fivefold from the period just following the Civil War to the present day, and its increase has been comparatively uniform for over six decades. However, annual fluctuations of the divorce rate are irregular, and the only declines have occurred during years of business depression presumably due to the costs of court fees The probability of divorce in this country at present is approximately 18 per cent for all marriages. If the national divorce rate continues to advance at the same uniform speed as occurred

138

DYNAMIC SOCIETY AND DIVORCE VELOCITY 139

during the past sixty-three years, then a trifle more than three decades hence would show the majority of American marriages ending in divorce.

Legal grounds for divorce fail to explain the wide divergence in state divorce rates between the eastern and western sections of the country. A summary analysis of the alleged legal causes of divorce indicates that about two-thirds of American divorces are included in that broad category classified as mutual incompatibility, while the remaining minority constitutes what may be termed grave causes of marital disruption.

The efforts to elucidate certain underlying conditions that operate in broken families as revealed in the contemporary divorce courts yield disappointing results due to a pronounced lack of clear factual evidence. Statements of judges and psychiatrists are contradictory as to current causes of divorce. The sole, outstanding factor upon which these opinions are corroborated by statistical evidence is the prevalence of divorce in cities. After legal, racial and religious conditions are taken into consideration, the urban divorce rate is probably twice that of rural areas. All statistical tests of variance indicated a decided heterogeneity of conditions related to divorce in different geographical sections of the country and an instability of underlying causes

In this entire sixty-three year period, the tendency of both marriage and divorce laws has been toward increasing strictness, but the divorce rate has steadily advanced, showing only negligible effects of legal changes. The exaggerated bogey of migratory divorce probably accounts for only 3 per cent of the grand total. Furthermore, a federal divorce law by constitutional amendment would be a dogmatic but futile standardization of this family problem. Perhaps about a third of divorced people rewed, or a rate of remarriage not much higher than for widowed persons.

140 STATISTICAL ANALYSIS OF AMERICAN DIVORCE

Fewer children and briefer marriages are two trends positively associated with divorce. Divorce is not an American family habit because five cases in every six come from that small class of American marriages bearing no children or but one child The diminishing size of the family presents a marked manifestation of its declining cohesiveness. Children preserve the home since only 8 per cent of American married couples possessing children end in the divorce court, while 71 per cent of the childless marriages terminate in divorce Furthermore, every additional child cuts in half the chances of divorce. Likewise the shortening duration of these marriages where the home is eventually broken is a distinct trend that has paralleled the increasing divorce rate, the fourth year of married life now being the most common for divorce, as compared with the seventh year at an earlier period.

Finally, any statistical study of divorce by quantitative methods cannot hope to evaluate all the factors which contribute to the increasing divorce rate. Many are so closely blended that they could not be distinguished as individual factors. A plausible cause of increasing divorce, as the growth of individualism, is not directly measurable by any statistical index. Such a problem in human motives at present remains unmeasurable and beyond the resources of quantitative methods.

Among the intangible but persistent causes of increasing divorce cited by previously quoted authorities was societal decay as instanced by the growth of crime and insanity. No concrete evidence is available, as the only data on crime and insanity consist of records of inmates of institutions. Unfortunately, the number of internments in state prisons and asylums has for decades in this country depended not on the amount of crime and insanity but on the space available in these over-crowded institutions. Thus the trend of social

DYNAMIC SOCIETY AND DIVORCE VELOCITY   141

degeneracy cannot on any reliable basis be numerically compared with the trend of the increasing divorce rate.

Religious decline as another intangible cause of increasing divorce has been previously discussed   The consistent advance in church membership in the United States, augmenting at the same rate as the total population, casts doubt on any premature conclusion as to the effect of declining religion upon increasing divorce.   However, church membership data are hardly a real index of spiritual influence, so this causal factor must be considered as unmeasurable.

One prominent factor mentioned, which likewise cannot be measured is the growing social approval of divorce. During the entire sixty-three year yeriod, divorce has become gradually less and less of a social stigma and a public blemish   This is merely due to the influences of habit and imitation. /The more divorces there are, the less unpopular it becomes with people in general, and taboos are gradually broken down.   Still further increases in divorce modify the community mores on the subject.   Thus it is evident that every divorce is in some way influenced by the number of divorces preceding it.   The matter simply is that divorce is a function of its own increase, and perhaps this helps to explain the prolonged uniformity in the rate of divorce increase.

This brief review of the available facts concerning increasing divorce does not present any simple explanation of the problem.   It is too closely interwoven with a complexity of changing relationships in the rapidly advancing American civilization since the years just following the Civil War.   A passage written two decades ago by Professor Lichtenberger is still appropriate:

The period of the rapid rise of the divorce rate has been one of transition; that the phenomena we are studying are due in a large measure to the fact that the world moves forward.   No

142 STATISTICAL ANALYSIS OF AMERICAN DIVORCE

one, we think, will question the ultimate advantage to society of the largest possible achievement in industrial efficiency, in individual and social freedom, and in ethical culture. These unquestionably minister to human welfare and to the growth of personality. They are elements of social solidarity, not of social degeneracy. The difficulties arise not out of the nature, but out of the rapidity of the movement. Velocity creates friction. Developments have been so rapid as to throw society out of adjustment in many of its aspects . . . It is no more surprising that there should be disturbances in domestic circles, as a result of these transitions, than that there shall be turmoil in industrial and religious circles. Increased divorce, therefore, appears clearly in the light of an effect rather than a cause. It is one of the " costs of progress." [1]

Thus the rapidity of increase in the American divorce rate is the product of changing social conditions. The equilibrium of the family institution has been shaken by the radical transformations in its economic and social environment.

[1] Lichtenberger, *Divorce a Study in Social Causation*, pp 211-212.

BIBLIOGRAPHY

Bates, Lindell T., *Divorce and Separation of Aliens in France*, Columbia University Press, New York 1929.

——, "The Divorces of Americans in Mexico," *American Bar Association Journal*, November, 1929, pp 709-713

Chaddock, Robert E, *Principles and Methods of Statistics*, Houghton Mifflin Co, Cambridge, Mass., 1925

Civic Federation of Dallas, *Divorce in Dallas*, Dallas. 1922.

Colcord, Joanna C., *Broken Homes*, William F Fell Co., Philadelphia 1919.

Corpus Juris, Vol. 19, American Law Book Co., New York, 1920.

Dike, Samuel W, *National League for the Protection of the Family Annual Report*, Boston, 1897.

——, "Sociological Notes: Marriage and Divorce," *Andover Review*, April, 1889, pp 427-433

——, "Statistics of Marriage and Divorce," *Quarterly Publications of the American Statistical Association*, March, 1889, pp. 206-214.

' Divorce," *Putnam's Magazine*, December, 1856, pp. 630-634.

Ellwood, Charles A., "Is the American Family to Die?" *Delineator*, February, 1909, pp 228-229

Ezekiel, Mordecai, *Methods of Correlation Analysis*, John Wiley and Sons. Inc., New York, 1930.

Groves, Ernest R. and Ogburn, William F., *American Marriage and Family Relationships*, Henry Holt & Co., New York, 1928.

Hartt, Rollin L., "The Habit of Getting Divorces," *World's Work*, August, 1924, pp. 403-409.

Hill, Joseph A. "Statistics of Divorce," *Quarterly Publications of the American Statistical Association*, June, 1909, pp. 486-504.

——, *Women in Gainful Occupations, 1870-1920*, Census Monograph ix, Government Printing Office, Washington. 1929

Howard, George E., *A History of Matrimonial Institutions*, vol. iii, University of Chicago Press, Chicago, 1904.

——, *The Family and Marriage*, University of Nebraska Press, Lincoln, 1914.

Johnsen, Julia E., *Selected Articles on Marriage and Divorce*, H. W. Wilson Co., New York, 1925.

Keezer, Frank H., *A Treatise on the Law of Marriage and Divorce*, second edition, Bobbs-Merrill, Indianapolis, 1923.

BIBLIOGRAPHY

Koehn, George L., "Is Divorce a Social Menace?" *Current History Magazine*, May 1922, pp. 294-299.

Library of Congress, Herman H. B. Meyer, Bibliographer, *A List References on Divorce*, Government Printing Office, Washington, 1915.

——, D G. Patterson, Bibliographer, *References on Divorce, 1915-1930*, mimeographed, Washington, 1930

——, W. A. Slade, Bibliographer, *A List of References on Uniform Divorce Laws*, mimeographed, Washington, 1925.

Lichtenberger, James P, *Divorce a Study in Social Causation*, Columbia University Studies in History, Economics and Public Law, vol. xxxv, New York, 1909

——. *Divorce*, McDraw Hill Book Co., New York, 1931.

Lotka. Alfred J., "Sterility in American Marriages," *Proceedings of the National Academy of Science*, January, 1928, pp. 99-109

Marshall Leon C., "A Statistico-Legal Study of the Divorce Problem," *Proceedings of the American Statistical Association*, March, 1931, pp. 96-106.

Massachusetts Annual Report of Vital Statistics, 1929, State Printing Office, Boston, 1930.

Mitchell, Wesley C., *Business Cycles, the Problem and Its Setting*, National Bureau of Economic Research, New York, 1928

Monthly Review of Credit and Business Conditions, Second Federal Reserve District, January, 1928, 1929, 1930, 1931

Mowrer, Ernest R, *Domestic Discord*, University of Chicago Press, Chicago, 1928.

——, *Family Disorganization*, University of Chicago Press, Chicago, 1927.

National Congress on Uniform Divorce Laws, Harrisburg Publishing Co., Harrisburg, 1906

National Desertion Bureau, *Report of the Desertion Committee*, Compiled from the Questionnaires, mimeographed, New York, 1928.

New Republic, "The Civilizing of Divorce," August 10, 1928, pp 266-267

New York State Department of Health Annual Report, 1912, Albany.

New York Times, Monthly Index, 1931.

Ogburn, William F, "The Changing Family," *Publications of the American Sociological Society*, October, 1929, pp. 124-133.

Parker, Franklin E, *Marriage and Divorce with a Soul Understanding*, Boston, 1923.

Patterson, S. Howard, "Family Desertion and Non-Support," *The Journal of Delinquency*, September, November, 1922, pp. 249-282.

Richmond, Mary E. and Hall, Fred S., *Marriage and the State*, Russell Sage Foundation, New York, 1929, pp. 299-333.

Rietz, Henry L., *Handbook of Mathematical Statistics*, Houghton Mifflin Co., Cambridge, Mass., 1924

BIBLIOGRAPHY

145

Ross, Edward A., *Changing America*, The Century Co, New York, 1912, Chapter iv.

Rubinow, Isidore M., "After Divorce—What?" *New Republic*, July 16, 1930, pp 226-228.

——, "Marriage Rates Increasing in Spite of Divorces," *Current History Magazine*, November, 1928, pp. 289-294

Sanctity of Marriage Association, Bulletin No. 8, 1923.

Snyder, Carl, *Business Cycles and Business Measurements*, The Macmillan Co., New York, 1927

Thomas, Dorothy S, *Social Aspects of the Business Cycle*, George Routledge and Sons, Ltd., London, 1925.

Truesdell, Leon E., *Farm Population of the U. S.*, Census Monograph vi, Government Printing Office, Washington, 1926.

Trumbull, Benjamin, *Unlawfulness of Divorce, An Appeal to the Public*, J. Meigs, New Haven, 1788.

"Uniform Marriage and Divorce Laws," *Congressional Digest*, June-July, 1927.

U. S. Birth, Still Birth, and Infant Mortality Statistics, 1928 (1929 mimeographed), Government Printing Office, Washington, 1930.

U. S. Census, 1890, vol 1, 1900, vol. i; 1910, vol. 1; 1920, vols. i, ii, iii; 1930, vol. i and press releases.

U. S. Census Abstract, 1920, Government Printing Office, Washington, 1923.

U. S. Census, *Prisoners 1923*, Government Printing Office, Washington, 1926

U. S. Census, *Religious Bodies*, 1926, Government Printing Office, Washington, 1930.

U. S. House of Representatives, *Adverse Report on House Resolution 46*, Fifty-second Congress, 1st Session, House Report 1290, May 5, 1892.

U. S Legislative Reference Bureau, *Index of State Laws, 1917-1928*. Library of Congress, Washington.

U. S. Life Tables, 1910, Government Printing Office, Washington, 1921.

U. S. Marriage and Divorce Report, 1867-1886, 1887-1906, 1916, 1922, 1923, 1924, 1925, 1926, 1927, 1928, 1929 (1930 press releases), Government Printing Office, Washington.

U. S. Statistical Abstract, 1926, 1930, Government Printing Office, Washington.

Waller, Willard, *The Old Love and the New*, Horace Liveright, New York, 1930.

Willcox, Walter F, "A Study in Vital Statistics," *Political Science Quarterly*, March, 1893, pp. 69-96

——, "Divorce in the United States," *Encyclopedia Britannica*, fourteenth edition, Encyclopedia Britannica Co, Ltd., London, 1929, vol. vni, pp. 459-460.

BIBLIOGRAPHY

——, "Notes on Divorce," *Quarterly Publications of the American Statistical Association*, March, 1914, pp. 483-485.

——, "Statistics of Marriage and Divorce in the United States," *International Statistical Institute*, Paris, 1909, pp 1-15.

——, "The Change in the Proportion of Children in the United States," *Quarterly Publications of the American Statistical Association*, March, 1911, pp. 490-499.

——, *The Divorce Problem, a Study in Statistics*, Columbia University Studies in History, Economics and Public Law, vol. i, New York, 1891.

Woollsey, Theodore D., *Divorce and Divorce Legislation*, second edition revised, C. Scribner's Sons, New York, 1882.

World Almanac, 1928, 1930, Press Publishing Co., New York.

World's Work, "Divorce, a Growing American Habit," December, 1926, p. 125.

Wright, Caroll D., *Outline of Practical Sociology*, seventh edition, Longmans, Green and Co., New York, 1909.

INDEX

Accuracy of data, 17, 19
Age of marriage, 81, 82, 121
Alimony, 43, 48, 61, 88
Annulment, 17, 71, 118

Bates, Lindell T., 64, 65
Benson, John G., 47
Bigamy, 42, 65
Birth rate, 62, 110-112, 129-132
Bi-serial r correlation, 82

Canada, 66, 67, 75
Chaddock, Robert E, 19
Childless marriages, 112-115, 137
Children, 43, 48-51, 62, 110-115,
    125, 127
Church membership, 57, 141
Coefficient of disturbancy, 21
Colcord, Joanna C., 16
Common-law marriage, 80, 83
Compromise legislation, 96, 97
Congressional divorce law, 73, 84,
    93-97
Connecticut, 53, 56, 70, 98, 99, 123
Contests, 43, 48
Correlation, 23, 53-56, 61, 82, 83,
    112, 135, 136
Costs, 49, 65, 77, 86, 126, 133, 136
Cruelty, 37, 39-43, 57, 84, 89

Davis, Katherine B, 47
Death of divorced persons, 29, 30,
    99, 101-109
Death of married couples, 29, 30,
    120-123
Decennial Census, 59, 60, 68, 81,
    99-109, 130
Definition, 15
Degeneracy, 46-49, 51, 53, 54, 62,
    79, 128, 140, 141
Denial of divorce, 48, 87
Depression, 77, 132-137
Derivation of divorce, 15
Desertion as ground for divorce,
    39-43, 49, 50, 55-57, 73, 84, 90

Desertion problem, 16, 17
Dike, Samuel W., 18, 63, 99 102,
    104
District of Columbia, 27, 53, 60,
    71-73, 77-79, 84, 85, 88, 94-97, 123
Divorce questionnaire, 17, 18
Drunkenness, 39-43, 47, 49, 84
Duration of marriage, 54, 115-125

Early divorce, 123-125
Eastern conservatism in divorce, 23,
    42, 53, 60, 91, 123
Ecclesiastical legislation, 55-57, 86
Economic and social causes, 20, 32,
    50, 53, 62, 109, ch. IX, 141, 142
Ellwood, Charles A., 110
Experimental laboratories, 96, 97
Extent of divorce, 15, 17
Ezekiel, Mordecai, 23

Felony, 42, 84
Ferris, Ralph H, 47
Foreign-born, 16, 32, 58-60, 118
Frequency curves, 116-123
Functions of the family, 50, 51, 57,
    127

Hall, Fred S, 81, 82
Hartt, Rollin L., 45-48, 51
Hickson, William J., 45, 46
Hill, Joseph A., 98, 102, 130, 133
Hoffmann, C. W, 46
Hoover, Herbert, 15, 17
Howard, George, 79, 80
Hull, Bradley, 48
Human nature, 42, 109, 140

Illegitimacy, 53
Increase of divorce, 21, 23, 25, 27,
    29-31, 59, 85, 86, 92, 97, 98, 109,
    125, chs IX, X
Individualism, 126, 128, 140
Infidelity, 37, 39, 40-43, 47, 55-57,
    69, 72, 73, 84, 85, 94, 96
Insanity, 42, 89, 90

INDEX

Intangible causes, 137

Judges, 43, 45-54, 57

Koehn, George L., 113

Laune, Ferris F., 113
Legislation on divorce, ch. iii, 53, 55, 61, ch. vi
Lexis ratio of dispersion, 91
Liberal divorce laws, 74-77, 79, 85, 89-91, 95-97
Lichtenberger, James P, 56, 86-88, 127, 128, 141, 142
Lobby, 27, 93, 94
Lotka, Alfred J, 113
Louisiana, 40-42, 53, 73, 74, 85, 89, 95, 97

Marriage laws, 63, 79-83, 86-88, 97
Marriage of unfit, 80-82
Marriage rate, 21, 86, 87, 125, 133
Massachusetts, 53, 56, 68, 112, 123
McGee, Leonard, 46, 47
Mexico, 64-66, 68, 69, 78
Migratory divorce, ch. v, 79, 84, 94, 95, 97
Migratory marriages, 80, 82, 83
Modal year of divorce, 117, 119, 121, 123
Mores, 37, 126, 128, 141
Morgan, William L., 46
Mowrer, Ernest R., 16, 43
Multiplicity of causes, 47, 48, 60, 137, 141
Mutual incompatibility, 42-44, 46-49

National Desertion Bureau, 16
National Divorce Reform League, 18
Neglect to provide, 39-43, 84
Negro, 58, 71
Nevada, 40, 53, 67-78, 84, 85, 90, 95, 97, 123
New Mexico, 40, 53, 56
Newspaper publicity, 49, 64, 76, 113
New York, 42, 53, 60, 61, 68-70, 72, 75, 77, 78, 85, 90, 95, 97, 101, 102, 123
North Carolina, 40, 42, 53, 70, 71, 73, 78, 85, 95, 97

Ogburn, William F., 23, 25, 50, 55, 57-61, 101, 102, 112, 115, 126, 127, 133

Omnibus clause, 84
Oregon, 74-77, 90, 95, 123

Paris, 64-66, 68, 69, 78
Parker, Franklin E., 93
Patterson, S. Howard, 16
Prophecies, 27, 29, 30
Poverty, 46-49, 51, 54, 55, 62
Probability of divorce, 15, 29, 30, 113-125
Protestants, 55-57
Psychiatrists, 49-54
Public opinion, 73, 85, 95, 97, 126
Putnam's Magazine, 64

Quotations from recent U S. Marriage and Divorce Reports, 32-34, 39, 66

Rate of divorce, 18, 19, 21, 23, 25, 29, 30, 33
Real causes of divorce, 17, 35, 39, ch. iv, 62, 91
Reconciliation, 50
Regularity of divorce increase, 21, 23, 30, 81, 136, 141
Religion, 32, 47, 51, 53, 55-57, 60-62, 91, 126-128, 141
Remarriage, 63, 79, 86-90, ch. vii
Residence requirements of states, 53, 75-77, 82, 84, 85, 87, 88, 90
Revenues from divorce, 73, 77
Rhode Island, 40, 53, 56, 92, 98
Richmond, Mary E., 81, 82
Roman Catholic, 34, 53, 55-57, 59, 60
Rome, 27, 29
Ross, Edward A., 23
Roosevelt, Theodore, 18, 93, 94
Rubinow, I. M., 102-109

Sabath, Joseph, 48-51
Saturation point of divorce increase, 23, 25
Secrecy of divorce, 77, 89
Separation, 15
Snyder, Carl, 129, 130, 134, 135
South Carolina, 53, 70-72, 84, 85, 95, 97
Standard area map, 53, 83
Standard error of the difference, 19
Standard of living, 54
State divorce rates, 23, 25, 27, 29, 32
States with decreasing divorce, 25, 27

INDEX 149

Statistical approach, 20, 53, 61, 62, 128, 129, 136, 137, 140
Statistical unit, 18, 19, 133
Stringent laws, 53, 60, 68, 70, 73, 74, 84, 89-92, 94-97
Summary, 138-140

Thomas, Dorothy S., 133
Truesdell, Leon E., 130
Trumbull, Benjamin, 27, 29
Truthlessness of divorce applicants, 46, 48

Underestimate of divorced persons in Decennial Census, 59, 100, 104-109
Uniform divorce laws, 53, 64, 79, 85, 92-97
Urbanization, 51, 57-60, 62, 129-132, 137

U. S. Legislative Reference Bureau, 89
U. S. Life Tables, 108, 121

Valid Causes, 42-44

Waller, Willard, 99, 102
War, 120, 136
Western frequency of divorce, 23, 32, 34, 42, 43, 53, 60, 66, 75, 91
Wife the divorce complainant, 48, 60, 61
Willcox, Walter F., 18, 29, 30, 64, 85, 86, 99, 102, 104, 112, 126, 127, 130, 132
Women wage-earners, 46, 50, 51, 61, 62, 129-133, 137
Woolsey, Theodore D., 18
World's Work editorial, 44
Wright, Caroll D., 18, 35, 64, 83
Wyoming, 75, 76, 123

CPSIA information can be obtained
at www.ICGtesting.com
Printed in the USA
LVHW080356180922
728633LV00031B/698